AMERICAN APARTHEID

AMERICAN APARTHEID

By
James S. Wright

ISBN: 1-4819-5107-6
ISBN-13: 9781481951074

Dedication/Acknowledgements

When the camera focuses on a ballplayer on the sidelines, the player usually takes that opportunity to say "Hello!" to family and friends. Now that I am in the spotlight, so to speak, I would like to say "Hello" to and dedicate my book to the following: my loving wife, Jackie, my wonderful children and grandchildren; my mother, Estelle Wright Thomas; my father, James S. Wright, Sr.; and my stepmother, Barbara Wright.

The first of many thanks is to God for providing me with the skills to write this book. The next most "thank you" is to my grandparents, Louanna and Wilbur Wright, who are the best role models a man could have.

Special thanks go also to one of my best friends, Priscilla Young, who along with Gene Noble, Gary Reynolds, Paul Evans, my publisher, Charles Lowder, the graphic artist, and Clifton Ball, helped make my dream come true.

Finally, a real big thanks to all of you who read this book. My next book, *American Apartheid: The Saga Continues*, will come along soon. I hope you will enjoy it too. Again, thank you.

We hold these truths to be self-evident that all men are created equal. That they are endowed by their Creator with certain inalienable rights. That among these are life, liberty and the pursuit of happiness.

From the Declaration of Independence

Contents

Introduction

The first question you probably asked when you picked this book is "Why the title *American Apartheid?*" Contrary to popular belief, books, as well as people, are judged by their first impressions or covers. A perfect example of this theory is the fact that you are about to read this book. The explanation for the title of the book will be made very clear as you continue to read it.

Let me give just a few facts about the author of this book. I am a forty-nine-year old African-American male. I was born in Dorsey, Maryland, a small rural community just outside of Baltimore. I was reared by my grandparents, who instilled in me a strong moral background, the foundation of which was religion and the church. I was educated in the local public schools. I did attend college, but I did not graduate. I am married and have three daughters and a son. I also have five grandchildren. I now live with my wife in Woodlawn, Maryland, a suburb of Baltimore. I believe in God. I love my family, and I think the United States of America is the best country in the world.

The next question you might ask is "Why did I write a book?" When asked why the man climbed the mountain, his response was because it was there. My answer to why I wrote this book is because it needed to be written. I joined the Marine Corps because I thought I could make a difference for my country. I became a police officer because I thought I could make a difference in my community. I wrote this book because I think it will make a difference in how Americans look at the topic of racism.

Yes, this book is about racism in America. I am quite sure you already figured that out when you read the title. The red, white and black colors on the book cover represent the three races of people that make up the history of this country.

This book does not contain any unknown facts or discoveries. Most of the information in this book is common knowledge. What this book does contain is a very fresh and very opinionated perspective on the subject of American racial equality.

My purpose in writing this book is to jump-start the stalled vehicles that drove Americans to the battleground where the war for racial equality was fought in this country. For the past 15 years or so, the Civil Rights Movement, which was very aggressive in the 1960's and 1970's, has slowed to a crawl. The fight for racial equality is far from over. Hopefully, this book will inspire a rebirth of the Civil Rights Movement.

The opinions in this book are supported by my Constitutional rights under the First Amendment, which guarantees freedom of speech and freedom of the press. What makes this book unique is that my opinions are very close to, and may even be, the actual facts. This book also presents a different account of American history. My opinions of U.S. history may not be the same as the lessons you learned in grade school, but they will be just as interesting.

This is not a textbook. The historical events described in this book did actually happened. My account of what may or may not have happened before and after these recorded events in history is my opinion. If you are looking for accurate dates and times when these historical events actually occurred, I suggest you check some reference books in your local library. There will be no footnotes that give the reference material used to make some of the statements you read. This is not a term paper or a thesis. This book is a wake-up call for those of us who have gone to sleep on the problem of racism in America.

I hope you will enjoy reading my book as much as I have enjoyed writing it.

Chapter One

It is my opinion that, aside from the treatment of the Jews during the Holocaust, the most tragic case of man's inhumanity to man is the treatment of the Native American people in the United States. The Native Americans were also the first American victims of apartheid. Third on my list would be the enslavement of my ancestors, the African Americans, by white Americans.

You might think that, as an African American, I would feel slavery was man's greatest inhumanity to man. Although the enslavement of my ancestors by white Americans was appalling, it pales in comparison to the Holocaust and the injustices endured by the Native Americans. The concept of slavery is as old as time itself, and, in most cases, it did not result in one race of human beings enslaving another race of human beings. Slavery was usually the result of the strong enslaving the weak for social or economic reasons.

The enslavement of Africans in America was not the white man's first attempt at slavery. Long before the black man was brought to America, the white man made an attempt to make the red man his slave; however, the free spirit of the Native Americans would never allow them to be slaves. When the white man attempted to put the Native Americans in bondage, they simply died. Without their freedom, the

Native Americans lost the will to live. This will give you some idea of why they fought so hard to keep their land and their freedom in this country.

During World War II, Adolph Hitler, the self-proclaimed Supreme Commander of the German Army, attempted to exterminate all the Jews in Europe. As part of his plan to establish a master race, Hitler, who may have been a Jew himself, ordered his troops to herd all the Jews in Germany into concentration camps and kill them. The Jews who were not killed in these camps had to endure the pain of seeing their family members and friends put to a horrible death in gas chambers. This is a very short description of the Holocaust. It would take an entire book for me to express my anger and disgust regarding Hitler's treatment of the Jews in Germany.

Almost 50 years later, members of Hitler's general staff are still in prison, still going to trial and still being pursued for the crimes committed against Jews. So atrocious were the crimes Hitler committed against the Jews, that, periodically, people dug up Hitler's bones, moved them to another grave and buried them again. This is said to be done to make sure Hitler is dead and to ensure, even in death, he will never rest in peace. The world has not forgotten the heinous acts committed against the Jewish people during the Holocaust, and, in my opinion, it should never forget.

One of the main reasons the world cannot forget the Holocaust is that there are thousands of Jews still living today who were actual victims of this inhumane treatment. The Jews who survived the Holocaust can give accurate eyewitness accounts of the crimes committed by Hitler and his troops. These survivors will never let the world forget for a moment what happened to Jewish citizens of Germany and other parts of Europe.

During the early development of the United States,

there were several attempts to exterminate the Native Americans. They were not put in concentration camps, but they were slaughtered and driven from their homes. The need for more space for white settlers coincided with the increased aggression by whites against the Native Americans. The red man was pushed off his land or killed to make room for the foreign invaders. In some states, the Native Americans were even hunted, and their scalps turned in for bounties.

The plight of the Native Americans in this country is what actually inspired the title of this book, *American Apartheid*. When Americans hear the word apartheid in this day and age, we immediately look at the situation in South Africa. Most of the free world countries, including the United States, have been very outspoken as to their opposition to apartheid in South Africa. Governments, private industries and human interest groups have all imposed some form of economic and social sanctions against South Africa for its practice of apartheid.

The cries to free Nelson Mandela, the black leader of the African National Congress, who was imprisoned in South Africa for his opposition to apartheid, were heard around the world. In 1990, Nelson Mandela was finally freed, and, in 1993, the former president, F.W. De Klerk, and Nelson Mandela were awarded the Nobel Prize for Peace for their efforts to end apartheid in South Africa. The efforts of President Nelson Mandela and former President De Klerk have led to a decrease in apartheid as of 1997.

Let us take a quick look at how I envision apartheid started in South Africa. White people moved from homes in their native country and decided to settle in South Africa. There is nothing wrong with moving to a new neighborhood and starting what could possibly lead to a better life for you and your family. The problems began when the white people, who just moved into the neighborhood, wanted to take

17

control of the entire country and the people who already lived there, who, in this case, just happened to be black.

Does this story sound familiar? It should sound familiar because our country was started in much the same way.

In 1492, Christopher Columbus sailed across the Atlantic Ocean from Spain and "discovered" America. It was called a discovery because Columbus represented the first "civilized" race of people to step foot onto the "New World." Because Columbus thought he had landed in the Indies, he named the native people who were already living in this new world "Indians."

Columbus claimed the "New World" for the Queen of Spain. This sounds like a game we used to play, "finders keepers, losers weepers." Hey Columbus, wake up and smell the coffee! The people whom you labeled Indians were here first. This "New World" you think you discovered was not yours to give away to anyone. The attitude displayed by Columbus represents another case of white people moving into a new neighborhood and taking over the entire country from the people who already lived there. In this case, the people happened to be red. This was the beginning of apartheid in America.

How did most Americans learn about the events surrounding the forming of our country? We all studied American history in school. As the pages of our history books were turned, we learned the basics about the discovery of America. It began with Columbus, followed later by Plymouth Rock, Pocahontus, John Smith, and, of course, Thanksgiving. The problem with the pages of history is they usually contain a very one-sided account of what actually happened. There is very little chance that the Native Americans' account of what took place when the Pilgrims landed at Plymouth Rock has ever been told.

18

History is like art. It is said that the beauty of art is in the eye of the beholder. The accuracy of the accounts of history is in the eyes of the reporters. Over the years, the accounts of established historical events have been changed. New documentation has been discovered that changed how history is to be recorded for events that date far beyond the discovery of America. History is also like gossip. You should never believe everything you hear or read about anything unless you actually witness the event yourself.

I am sure you have taken part in the classroom experiment that starts a story at one end of a line of students, and the story is passed on until it reaches the other end of the line. This classroom experiment always results in the original story never being the one you end with. History can be like a snowflake with no two accounts of history ever being the same, or it could be like peas in a pod and repeated accurately each time it is recalled. It is my opinion that the accounts of history are like the classroom experiment. Each time the accounts of history are passed on from one generation to another, the story changes.

The American history that was taught in American schools before the Civil Rights Movement was as much fiction as it was fact. The glaring flaw in how American history was taught in the school systems was that it was only taught in one color, and, in America, that color was white. Even before schools were integrated, the courses taught in black and red schools were controlled by a white male Board of Education. Therefore, black and red children were taught white history. There was no way the apartheid system of government would allow the history of America to be taught from a perspective other than that of white supremacy.

The problem with history being taught in one color is you only see history from one perspective. Not teaching accurate accounts of both African-American and Native-

American history to American youth was a mistake, and, although it was a mistake, very little was done to correct the situation until the Civil Rights Movement of the 1960's. I hope this book will cause readers to take a closer look at how history should be taught in schools. As parents and future parents, we must demand that history be taught in more than one color.

After years of pressure from black leaders and African-American communities, most school systems today use February, which has been designated as Black History month, to teach all students some form of black history and African-American culture. Although it does not come close to being a complete and accurate account of black history or African-American culture, it is progress, and a little knowledge could open the door to some amazing discoveries. I will expound on my opinions regarding the subject of black history and African-American culture as you continue to read this book.

What about Native American history? Why not have a Red History Month? When I was in grade school, we did attempt to study the history of the Native Americans. The lesson began with a study of the ancient Indian tribes. My only recollection of that history class is very limited. Although I was very young at the time, I can remember how fascinated I was by the beauty of the colorful costumes and the artwork of the ancient Aztec and Inca Indian tribes.

However, as a young child, I was also terrified as I sat and listened while my teacher described the barbaric religious rituals and customs of the Aztecs and Incas. The thoughts of a race of people who practiced human sacrifice and drank blood as part of a religious worship ceremony were horrible. Therefore, my first impressions of ancient Indian tribes were that they were an uncivilized race of people who dressed in colorful costumes. I hope you can forgive my stereotypical assessment. I was just a child.

The fact is the Native Americans of this country may not even be related to the Aztecs and Incas. Most white historians grouped the native tribes of Central America and South America with the native tribes of North America, and it was probably the first time the white man used the line, "Well, they all look alike, so they must be from the same family." In fact, it is more likely that Mexican Americans in this country are the direct descendants of the Aztecs and Incas.

History was quick to associate the barbaric religious customs of the Incas and Aztecs to the Native Americans, but what historians fail to mention on a regular basis is the fact that the ancient Indian tribes were responsible for providing North America with such commonly used items as: the calendar, mathematics, pottery and architecture. Prior to the Civil Rights Movement, the powerful apartheid government could not allow its school systems to teach any history that might imply the Native American was more intelligent and, therefore, may be superior to the white man.

I also remember that we briefly studied the "American Indian." The studies mainly consisted of the distinctions between the Western or Plains Indian tribes and the Eastern Indian tribes. As a result of my grade school history, I was able to remember a few names of famous Native-American tribes. Most of the Native-American history taught in this country was closely associated with events that affected the white population of America. Native Americans are always mentioned in connection with Thanksgiving, the Northwest Passage, the French and Indian War and, of course, Custer's Last Stand.

However, there was one part of Native-American history that I did not need my grade school lessons to recall. The names of the great American Indian chiefs were always on the tip of my tongue. I learned the names of the great chiefs by watching hours of television every Saturday morning for about six years when I was young. The great Native-American chiefs dominated the movie and the television shows about the Old West. In my opinion, Chief Sitting Bull, Cochise, Ten Bears, Geronimo and Quanta Parker were just as popular as Daniel Boone, Davy Crockett, George Armstrong Custer, Wild Bill Hickok and Buffalo Bill Cody. Like most of the kids of my generation, I thought playing cowboys and Indians was as American as apple pie. It was one of my favorite pastimes, and I always wanted to play the Indian because I got to dress better than the cowboys.

In the movies and on television, the Indian was portrayed as a savage animal who slaughtered and raped innocent white women and children. In most of the early movies, the white male hero always came to the rescue and saved the white women and children and defeated the Indians. There were very few occasions in the movies that the Indian was portrayed as a hero. If you think this was done by accident, then you believe in Santa Claus. The fact that the Native American was rarely portrayed as the hero in the movies was part of the scheme to endorse the idea of apartheid in America.

When you mention the names of white movie stars like John Wayne and Errol Flynn, most of my generation will immediately associate them with America's Western heroes. There are, however, probably few Americans from my generation who can remember Native-American movie stars such as Jay Silver Heels, better known as "Tonto," and Chief Iron Eye Cody, who probably appeared in as many movies about the Old West as John Wayne and Errol Flynn. What harm would it have done if Hollywood made a few more movies that put the Native Americans in starring roles and made them the heroes?

Even in the games we played as children, the Indians

always lost. Now that I am older, I often wonder if young Native American children played cowboys and Indians, and, if they did, I wonder who won? Now that I am older, I really feel sorry for the Native-American children who may never have gotten to know the true history of their race. Now that I am older, I also feel really cheated because I was never taught the true history of some of my childhood heroes, the great Native American chiefs.

One of the main reasons apartheid still exists in South Africa, is successful in America, and was a contributing factor to the defeat of the Native Americans in this country, is called genocide. Rather than band together as one race, the Native-American tribes and native African tribes in South Africa fought wars against each other. Not only did the natives of these two countries fight wars among themselves, they joined the army of the white government and helped the white man take their land and kill members of their own race. Native Americans killing Native Americans. Native Africans killing native Africans. Us killing us. That is genocide. Please remember the term "genocide" because it still exists today in America, and it is just as destructive as ever.

As an African American, one of the most appalling and noticeable conditions surrounding apartheid in South Africa is the number of black soldiers in the South African army. Black troops are used to enforce apartheid. I watched televised news reports and witnessed black South Africans being beaten and killed because they protested the practice of apartheid. The sight of black protestors being beaten by black soldiers was sickening. Later in this book, I will continue to discuss my total contempt for the practice of apartheid by the South African government.

America is extremely proud of its democratic system of government. This democratic system of government that we, as Americans, are so proud of was adopted from the

Native-American tribes. The early white European settlers discovered the Native-American tribes elected their leader based on the number of good deeds that the tribesman had done for his people. Prior to the Civil Rights Movement, white historians would never let it be known that the so-called savage Indians practiced a democratic form of government in this country before the white man. This is another case of the "good old boys" not wanting it publicized that the democratic system of government that we hold so dear was the product of the Native Americans.

The American democratic system of government is run by the people, for the people, and is based on the majority rules. As Americans, we know how majority rule works. For example, the majority political party rules Congress and helps govern this nation. However, if the majority were destined to rule in America, why did the Native Americans lose this country to the white man? Another long-established rule in this country is that possession is nine-tenths of the law. In that case, what gave the white man the right to claim this country from the Native Americans who were already here?

How could the white man find the audacity to develop a system of apartheid in America and expect for this system to be accepted by the Native Americans who had lived here for 1,400 years? Just imagine how you would feel if a group of strangers knocked at your door, invited themselves in, sat and had dinner, and then told you to find a new home. That is basically what white Americans did to the Native Americans. White historians would have us believe that the early white American settlers first fought with the red man strictly as a means of survival. Most of us assume the white settlers, who were far outnumbered by the red man, were merely trying to establish themselves in the New World, and the Native Americans wanted to make sure the foreign invaders stayed in one area. Did the Native Americans start the war with the white man that would eventually lead to the destruction of their race in America? I think it was the need to conquer, as well as the "pioneer spirit," that first drove the white man into "Indian Territory."

The history of the world is full of conquests. One civilization after another has fought wars with other civilizations, and to the victor went the spoils. Wars fought during ancient history had very little to do with a man's race or the color of his skin. In the Old World, wars were fought to gain land, wealth and to establish religious doctrines. The more land and wealth one had, the more power and influence one had.

Although I compare the plight of the Native Americans to that of the Jews during the Holocaust, the Native American did have some control over his destiny in America, whereas the Jews had very little control of their destiny in Germany during World War II. Hitler's plan to create a "master race" by exterminating the Jews caught them by surprise. The Jews had very little time to mount a defense before they were herded into cattle cars and imprisoned in concentration camps. During the Holocaust, the Jews banded together and used whatever means available to fight the Nazis. They remained united throughout the horrors of the Holocaust. On the other hand, the Native Americans played a major role in assisting the white man to defeat them.

The Indian wars were a match-up of the white settlers, who were the minority, against the Native Americans, who were the majority. The world's long history of war will support the fact that, under most circumstances, the majority has always defeated the minority. How was it that, in this case, the white man managed to beat the odds and defeat the red man in this country? Well, if you believe most of the published accounts of American history, the white man

25

defeated the Indians because they were just plain smarter than the Native Americans. Those of you who support American Apartheid certainly agree with this rationale.

The fact that the Native Americans trusted the white man, which was their first mistake, was one of the main reasons they were defeated by the white man. The white man would betray their trust and become their worst enemy. The first Native-American tribes in this country were peace loving farmers. The red man shared his knowledge of farming with the white settlers, which enhanced the white man's ability to survive. The Native Americans were the first to develop popular American crops such as corn, squash, peppers, pumpkins, peanuts, sweet potatoes and white potatoes. They were also responsible for discovering chocolate and vanilla. Kids of today probably think Mr. Baskin and Mr. Robbins created these two favorite flavors.

It was not the Native Americans who started the war between the red man and the white man. The Native Americans welcomed the white settlers to share their land. The operative word here is "share" the land and its natural resources. The early Native-American tribes were community-minded people who believed in sharing all their possessions. It was the white settlers, with their apartheid mentality, who created an adversarial atmosphere between the white man and the Native Americans.

According to history, the so called "pioneer spirit" was so strong in the white settlers that it drove them to see what was over the next mountain and on the other side of the next river. The white man moved farther and farther into territory that, by all rights, belonged to the Native Americans. Actually, it was the selfishness of the white settlers that led to the abuse of the land and natural resources that the Native Americans depended on to survive. The defense of their land and its resources is what caused the initial conflicts between the Native Americans and the white Americans. The Native Americans' attempts to defend their land caused the white settlers to form a militia to protect them as they continued to take land from the Indians.

The early abuse of the natural resources in this country by the white man almost ruined the balance between man and nature that existed in America before the white man arrived. The Native Americans have a great respect for the land and all living creatures. The Native Americans only took from the land what they needed to survive and only killed animals for food and clothing. The white man made a business out of the trapping and killing of animals for their skins. After it was no longer profitable as a business, the white man killed animals as a sport.

This senseless killing of animals led to the near-extinction of the beaver, the red fox and that symbol of America, the bald eagle. The animal most abused by the white man in America was the buffalo. The Native Americans depended on the buffalo as their main source of meat. They wore the buffalo skins in the Winter to keep them warm and used the bones of the buffalo to make strong tools and weapons.

The white man first hunted the buffalo for the same reasons as the Native Americans. After cattle took the place of the buffalo on the dinner table, and cowhide leather became the new fashion, the only reason the white man continued to kill the buffalo was because they were a popular trophy for rich white people. White buffalo hunters would kill buffalo by the thousands, remove the heads and skins and leave the rest of their bodies to rot on the Western plains.

In all the movies I watched about the "Old West," I remember the Native Americans always were upset at the white man for killing buffalo. I even remember a movie called the "Buffalo Hunter." In this movie, you would see the men shoot the buffalo, the camera would move to the next scene, and another buffalo would be shot. As a child, I thought the men were good marksmen, and they also looked like they were having fun. It was only after I saw the movie "Dances With Wolves" that I experienced the full impact of the buffalo being slaughtered. In one scene, buffalo had been killed by white hunters, and the heads and skins had been removed, leaving only the bloody flesh of the buffalo. The Native Americans hung their heads, and the white hero of this film turned his head in shame. It was truly a disgusting sight.

Now, in America, we have just as many groups that protest animal abuse as we do those who protest for equal rights. I love animals, but I love human beings a whole lot more. The preservation of animals and animal rights was important to the survival of this country when it was first founded by the Native Americans, and it is still important today. There was, however, a more important message that I got from the movie "Dances With Wolves." The central theme of the movie was that the most important rights in America are those of all human beings, regardless of color.

Back to the question, "Why did the white man defeat the Native Americans?" One of the main reasons the white army was able to defeat the Native Americans was the United States military leaders used some very unscrupulous tactics. American history records these tactics as being more cunning and smarter than the Indians'. The army also used whatever devious methods necessary to keep Native American tribes fighting among each other. This helped to make one of the best weapons used by the white army in its war to defeat the Indian, the Indian himself.

In an attempt to stop the wars between the white army and the red man, the government and the Native Americans entered into hundreds of treaties. The treaties were rarely enforced; therefore, they were never very effective. The "Great White Fathers," the name given to the politicians in Washington by the Indians, did very little to protect the rights of the Native Americans. The white man always found some reason to break the treaties and violate the rights and properties of the Native Americans. Treaties were supposed to have been broken in the name of the "American Pioneer Spirit," which created the uncontrollable desire in the white man to move west.

President Andrew Jackson failed to enforce an act of Congress, which made it illegal for the white man to trespass on Native-American land. It was President Jackson's opinion that "Indians" did not have any rights in this country. President Jackson, who was a notorious "Indian Fighter," even refused to order federal troops to protect the property of the Native Americans from being invaded by white settlers. President Jackson actually felt he was preserving the Native American tribes by coercing them to move from their homes, cross the Mississippi River and travel thousands of miles to settle on the Western plains.

The Native Americans had to either sell their land to the government for far less than it was worth or be forced off their land by the white settlers. Although President Jackson would not allow the military to protect the Native Americans, he was quick to order the army to stop small bands of angry Indians who were fighting the white settlers in protest of the loss of their land. President Jackson thought the move to the West would protect the Native Americans from being exterminated. The Native Americans who died on the journey from the Mississippi River to the Western plains, which was called the "Trail of Tears," would turn over in their graves if they knew that President Jackson was enshrined on the $20 bill.

Horace Greely, the great American editor, said, "Go

west, young man. Go west." So, of course, he should also be held responsible for the steady increase in the number of white settlers moving west. The more white people that moved to the West, the greater the need for additional resources to support this invasion. White people needed more crops, more cattle and, of course, more land to survive. Where did white settlers seem to always get more land when they needed it? They broke treaties and pushed the Native Americans off their land.

The truth of the matter is the treaties were broken more in the name of greed than the desire to move west. When white men discovered gold and other valuable minerals on Native American land, they wanted to keep it all for themselves rather than share the wealth with the Indians. Just think how rich the Native Americans would be today if they had been allowed to keep, or even share, the wealth from the minerals discovered on land they once owned.

Although the white settlers were never willing to share the wealth of this country with the Native Americans, they were, however, willing to share things that the Native Americans did not want and surely did not need. The white American settlers freely gave to the Native Americans some highly contagious diseases such as smallpox, dysentery and cholera. Thousands of Indians, who were unable to get proper medical treatment, died from the diseases they caught from the white man.

The Native Americans' struggle to keep their land and preserve their way of life was hopeless. Whenever they attempted to defend their rights and enforce the treaties by protecting their land from the white settlers, the government ordered the army to protect the white settlers, and the Indian wars began again. As the years passed, the number of white settlers increased, and the population of the Native Americans decreased. Countless numbers of white immigrants continued to pour into this country from all over Europe. It was the misfortune of the Native Americans not to have any red immigrants to help replenish their race.

Chapter Two

After the Civil War, thousands of former slaves traveled west to begin a new life. There were very few jobs available to African Americans after the Civil War. Black men joined the army to help fight the Indians. For the former slaves, being a soldier was a respectable profession, and the pay was good. The money earned from being in the army was used by African Americans to buy land and other goods and services needed to survive in the West. Although the African Americans may not have had the same motives as the white soldiers who fought and killed the Native Americans, it was the black soldier's duty as a member of the army to fight and kill the Indian.

Being a soldier in the army was the first time most black men had ever been paid or given any respect for a job well done. The former slaves were proud of their new professions, and they became model soldiers. Although the white army may have admired the black soldiers, even dressed them in the same uniforms and gave them the same training as white soldiers, the white army made it quite clear that the African-American soldiers were in no way equal to the white soldiers.

White and black soldiers did not eat together, sleep in the same barracks and very seldom fought in the same battles. The white man tolerated the African Americans in the army because at the time they considered the former slaves the lesser of two evils. The other evil in this case was the Native American. The government, by enlisting the services of African Americans in its battle against the Indians, defeated the Native Americans without having to sacrifice additional white troops.

If fighting with the white man against the Native Americans would have improved the relationship between blacks and whites after the Civil War, I would have agreed that the African Americans did the right thing by joining the army. However, after the Indians had been defeated by the army, the African Americans became the white man's primary target for racial hatred and bigotry in America. Again, the word genocide surfaces. Us killing us, the red and black men killing each other for the benefit of the white man.

I am pleased to report that all the early contact between the Native Americans and the "Buffalo Soldiers" did not always result in bloodshed. Buffalo soldier is the name given to the black soldiers by the red man because the coarse hair and dark skin reminded the Native Americans of the buffalo. While studying African-American history and the development of the Western America, I found evidence that the Native American and African Americans did form a bond in parts of the Old West.

The fact that both races had been oppressed by the white man created a kindred spirit between the red man and black man. There are many families today that are the product of the interracial relationships between Native Americans and African Americans. I am proud to say that I have a great-great grandmother who was a slave and a great-great grandmother who was a full-blooded Cherokee.

As the children and grandchildren of slaves in this country, African Americans should have been very sympathetic to the plight of the red man. The Native Americans have a longer history of being the victims of racial discrimination than any other race of people in America. The Native Americans and African Americans need to rekindle the kindred spirit that was established after the Civil War.

By not actively including the Native Americans in their fight for racial equality, the African Americans were just as guilty as the white man in making the red man the forgotten race in the United States. Although there has been a great deal of progress in the area of racial discrimination in America, the fight for civil rights and racial equality is a continuing battle. African Americans in the United States need to remember something: In order to win the war for racial equality, we need to enlist all the soldiers we can find. Red, yellow, black and brown men must remain united in the struggle for racial equality because, if we are divided, we will surely fall.

By the late 1860's, the Native Americans went from the vast majority to the minority race in the United States. The end of the Civil War in 1865 marked the beginning of the end of the great Native American tribes in this country. After the Civil War, the Union army and the former Confederate troops combined to fight the war against the Indians. As a result of constant fighting and their battle with contagious diseases, the population of the Native Americans, like the buffalo, was reduced to near-extinction. In 1875, the last of the warring Native American tribes surrendered, and the Indian Wars were finally over.

After centuries of being the dominant race in this country from sea to shining sea, the government forced the Native Americans to live on reservations. The Jews had to suffer through the horrors of concentration camps, and the Native Americans had to suffer through the humiliation of being confined to living on reservations. Most of the Indian reservations were located on desolate parcels of land in the mid-West. The government was willing to allow the Native Americans to live on land that no white man wanted.

The government created the Indian Affairs Agency as part of the Department of the Interior. The department, which ironically is also responsible for the protection of the environment and the preservation of wildlife in the United States, was assigned the task of ensuring the welfare of the Native Americans. In my opinion, the government actually created the Indian Affairs Agency in order to maintain control and closely monitor the Native Americans. The newly-formed Indian agency treated the Native Americans like little children. The Native Americans were told what, when and where to do everything. The great and powerful Native American chiefs, who were once feared and respected by the white man, had been stripped of their dignity and now reduced to taking orders from government-appointed white Indian agents.

You would think that, since a special agency of the government had been created to protect the Indians, they would have been safe, but the white man would never let the Native Americans have any peace. They raided the Indian reservations, destroying crops and stealing cattle. If the white men found anything of value on a reservation, they simply notified their representative in Congress, and the government would direct the Native Americans to move to another location. As the many years of war and disease killed the body of the Native Americans, life on the reservation killed their spirit.

The history of wars by the United States includes, but is not limited to, the following: the French and Indian War, the Revolutionary War, the War of 1812, the Civil War, the Mexican War and World War I and World War II. For all you Rough Riders who charged up San Juan Hill, and for the

Korean War and Viet Nam War veterans, I personally feel you fought in a war, but history calls them "police actions," so I did not include them on this list. After each of the wars listed, the country or countries the United States fought against and defeated managed to recover. Treaties were signed and never broken.

The United States spent millions of dollars to reconstruct the South after the Civil War and even sent millions of dollars overseas to help rebuild Germany after World War II. After dropping two atom bombs on Japan to help end World War II, America's guilty conscience resulted in millions of dollars being sent to Japan. What happened to the war relief for the Native Americans? Should America have made some attempt to reconstruct the "Indian Nation"?

The Native Americans have never recovered from the wars they fought and lost. Why did the government fail to provide funds to restore the Native Americans' way of life? During World War II, out of the fear of espionage and sabotage being committed in this country, the government ordered Japanese-born Americans and German-born Americans living in this country confined to concentration camps. After the war was over, the concentration camps in the United States were closed, and the Japanese and German Americans were allowed to live wherever they wanted. Why is it that in a country that is supposed to be the home of the brave and the land of the free, the Native Americans are still living on reservations? What happened to America's conscience when it came to helping them?

The world will never forget the war crimes committed against the Jews during the Holocaust. Americans should never forget the war crimes committed against the Native Americans during the Indian Wars. There should be no statute of limitations on the crimes committed against the red man in this country. Unlike the war crimes committed by the Nazis against the Jews during World War II, white American history did not record the injustices suffered by the Native Americans at the hands of the government as war crimes.

Both Germany and Japan were left with permanent scars from their wars with the United States, but, with the help of the financial aid provided by American tax dollars, both countries recovered and now have thriving economies. Since most of the foreign cars sold in America are imported from Japan and Germany, the United States continues to support two countries who were at one time our bitter enemies. At one point in time, all a struggling country had to do was lose a war to the United States, and America would support it for the next 40 years.

My estimate is that, for every one dollar in tax revenue the government has spent in the past, or will spend in the future on Native American relief, a million dollars has been sent to foreign countries for some form of relief. Think about the billions of dollars the United States spends on imported goods rather than explore the possibility of allowing the Native Americans, or other minorities, to produce the same products locally and benefit from the profits.

Much of the recognition for the success and early development of this country is given to the "American Pioneers." The credit for the survival of the early American settlers and pioneers belongs to the Native Americans. The problem is history has never given the Native Americans the credit they deserve for the role they played in the development of America. The white man was given credit for all the skills he learned from the Indians as well as all the tools and other inventions that originated from the Native-American culture.

The only recognizable attributes that the white man managed to give the Native Americans that are remembered

37

are uncomplimentary stereotypes. When Columbus "discovered" America and found the native people were not Christians, they were branded as being savages and totally uncivilized. This was the first of many stereotypical descriptions of the Native Americans. How could Columbus, or any of the other European settlers, call the Native Americans uncivilized when they knew nothing about them? The only thing they knew for sure about the so-called Indians was they were different. The brand of being savages stuck to the Native Americans throughout history, and it became very difficult to make a positive first impression when most white people viewed the red man as being uncivilized.

Some modern day negative terms that are commonly associated with the Native Americans such as "The only good Indian is a dead Indian," "Indian blankets," "Indian beads," the "Indian Rain Dance," and "Red Man Chewing Tobacco" do very little to remove the old stereotypes. In my opinion, the worst of this stereotypical behavior by Americans is the use of Native American names and customs as nicknames for athletic teams.

Without any consideration as to how the Native Americans might feel, athletic teams and their mascots in this country were nicknamed after a race of people. Because of the lack of respect for the Native Americans in the United States, most white Americans do not see the harm in this age-old tradition. Some Americans seem to feel they honor the Native American each time they do a "tomahawk chop" at a football game or baseball game. The Atlanta Braves, Cleveland Indians and Florida Seminoles are all teams nicknamed after the Native American. The most disrespectful of all these team nicknames is the Washington "Redskins." For a National Football League team located in the nation's capital to be nicknamed after a race of people is totally inappropriate.

Just think how America would react today if the

Washington "Redskins" were nicknamed the Washington "Jews" or Washington "Negroes." I do not think those nicknames would go over real big with the Jewish stockholders who invest in professional football or with African-American players who make up over 50 percent of the National Football League. What these examples truly represent is a strong argument for change. The next time you see a group of Native Americans protesting these racially offensive nicknames, why not lend your support? Let us give the Native Americans the respect they deserve and find some other nicknames for our athletic teams and mascots.

Not only is the use of the Native American culture as nicknames for athletic teams unethical, it also dishonors Jim Thorpe, a Native American, who was, beyond a shadow of a doubt, the greatest athlete who ever lived. In this day and age of Michael Jordan, Bo Jackson, Wayne Gretsky and Larry Bird, it might be hard for you to believe that Jim Thorpe could be the greatest athlete of all times—even greater than Babe Ruth, Mickey Mantle, Jim Brown and Johnny Unitas. Jim Thorpe accomplished more in his athletic career than any other athlete in history.

While attending a small college in Pennsylvania, Jim Thorpe lettered in football, baseball and track. He was an All-American football player and won an Olympic Gold Medal by winning the decathlon. He played professional baseball and made it into the Hall of Fame as a professional football player. Jim Thorpe did for Native Americans in this country what Jackie Robinson did for African Americans. Both men opened doors that had been closed to athletes of their respective races for generations.

Jim Thorpe went to Greece to represent the United States and won a Gold Medal in the Olympic decathlon. His accomplishments as an athlete should have been the opening line for a Pulitzer Prize-winning story. Unfortunately, the story of Jim Thorpe does have not have a happy ending. He died a poor man and never realized any of the fame and fortune usually associated with athletes of his stature. The downfall of Jim Thorpe is a classic case of a member of a minority race being let down by the white male establishment that controls this country.

After winning the Gold Medal, Jim Thorpe should have been exalted for his efforts and received a hero's welcome when he returned to his native land. White American winners of this Olympic event have been given the title "World Greatest Athlete" and went on to very successful careers. You might remember Bob Richards, America's Gold Medal winner in the decathlon. He was the first American Olympic decathlon winner to have his picture on the Wheaties cereal box, and the slogan "Breakfast of Champions" helped to make him rich and famous. Another American Olympic decathlon winner was Bruce Jenner, and he became an American sex symbol and millionaire. He appeared in several movies and did television sports commentary. Prosperity was not to be the reward for victory in the case of Jim Thorpe.

Aside from not reaping the benefits normally afforded an Olympic Gold Medal winner, Jim Thorpe was stripped of his Gold Medal by the Olympic Rules Committee shortly after his return to the United States. It seems the Olympic Rules Committee declared him to be a professional athlete and ineligible to compete in the Olympic games. Rather than support this great athlete in his battle to retain his Gold Medal, America turned its back and made Jim Thorpe the target for ridicule and shame.

During a Summer break from college, Thorpe and some other athletes from his school took jobs working on a farm. The owner of the farm also sponsored a semi-pro baseball team. After working on the farm all day, the workers played on the farmer's team. They were paid for working on the farm and not for playing baseball. The Olympic Rules Committee decided that, because the farm and the baseball team had the same owner, part of Jim Thorpe's job was to play baseball. As a result of this decision, Jim Thorpe was declared a professional athlete and stripped of his Olympic Gold Medal.

The Olympic Games should be just what the name implies "games," games in which men and women from different countries from all over the world get to play. Every race, color and creed of athlete is represented in these events, but the Olympics are not just games. The Olympics are a forum for political ideology. With every victory, and with each medal, the winning country takes the platform to make a political statement. Jim Thorpe got caught up in the politics of the Olympics, and it was a game even a great athlete could not win.

He did not have the expertise or the resources to fight the political system that had stripped him of his Gold Medal and his dignity. In order to win at the game of politics, one needs to be a politician. Our nation's capital is full of politicians, but they did not respond to the cry for help from Thorpe. In my opinion, the reason they did not respond is because he was an Indian. Had Thorpe been a white man, it would have been a different story. It would have been a sign of weakness for America to allow a white American hero to be dishonored. After years of battling the system, Thorpe's Olympic Gold Medal was returned, and his name returned to the Olympic Record Book. Another case of much too little being much too late. I am very thankful for the memory of Jim Thorpe.

Did you ever ask yourself this question: "Why did the Civil Rights Movement in this country fail to include the Native Americans?" History details certain monumental

41

events that broke down the barriers of discrimination in America. The Emancipation Proclamation marked the end of slavery in states still in rebellion, the Women's Suffrage Act gave females the right to vote, and the Civil Rights Bill of 1964 provided equal justice for the minority races in the United States. The only legislation that I can associate with the Native Americans are the rules and regulations that Congress enacted to govern the newly-formed Department of the Interior.

I remember Dr. Martin Luther King and Malcolm X as they led the struggle by African Americans for civil rights. I also remember all the freedom marches and speeches by our black leaders during the battle for equality. I can remember that, during the Civil Rights Movement of the 1960's, black leaders were supported by leaders from the Jewish and Hispanic communities who were also victims of racial discrimination. I remember these events because I lived through them. What I cannot remember is any mention of the discrimination being suffered by the Native Americans during this same period. The Native Americans, who once roamed this country as free as the American eagle, seem to be the forgotten race in America.

I am very proud of the fact that documentation was finally published that chronicled the role of African Americans in the Revolutionary War, the fight for this country's independence and freedom from England, and the Civil War, the battle between the states that ended slavery in America. I am not, however, proud of the role African Americans played in the white man's war against the Native Americans.

It simply staggers me when I think about the fact that Native Americans in the year 2000 will still be living on reservations. It is even more staggering when you realize that the Native Americans established the concept of community-living. Today's modern apartment houses were designed after the Pueblo tribes of the southwest. How many of us even bother to think of the Native Americans when we enter an apartment or use the term "community"? The apartheid conditioning by white America has not allowed the promotion of the Native Americans in a positive light.

Take a moment and think about it. Who actually benefits from having almost an entire race of people isolated on a reservation? The answer is the government. Why? Just take a look one day at all the research papers and other documentation that has been compiled about the Native American in the Library of Congress. These studies are based on the Native Americans' life style on the reservation.

Some examples of government studies that have been conducted using the Native Americans include: the learning ability or disability of the Native Americans, the rate of alcoholism among Indians, and do Indians have a higher rate of suicide than any other race? I compare this to studying fish in a fish bowl or animals in a zoo. I would be very supportive of these studies that were conducted by the government if the data collected were used to improve the life style of the Native Americans who still live on reservations.

If one would read the research material from a government study on the Native Americans, there is very little chance that you would get the full impact of the documentation. For example, I seriously doubt that the data collected on alcohol abuse by the red man will explain that the white man provided the whiskey, which was the major contributing factor that helped to spread this disease among Native Americans. There is an old saying in this country that, if someone calls you a bird often enough, you start to believe that you can fly. The white man created the stereotype that Native Americans have no tolerance for alcohol. After years of listening to white America refer to most Indians as drunks, combined with the depression created by living on reservations, Native Americans have, at times, turned to alcohol as an escape from reality.

Since the days of Columbus, the American settlers made a profit by using cheap whiskey to trade for goods and services from the Native Americans. There was a time in this country when it was illegal for a white man to sell alcoholic beverages to a Native American. Although it was illegal, the white man ignored the law and continued to sell cheap whiskey to the red man. This same scenario is being played out today. The sale of narcotics and controlled dangerous substances is illegal in the United States, but the white man breaks the law and continues to make a profit from the sale of illegal drugs.

Heroin and cocaine addiction is destroying African-American communities the same way that alcohol, the drug of choice for the red man, destroyed Native-American communities, while the white man continues to make a profit from the sale of drugs and alcoholic beverages. The government did very little to control the illegal sale of alcohol to the Native Americans by the early American pioneers, and it does very little today to keep the white man from selling illegal drugs in the black community. As long as crime and violence associated with alcohol and drug abuse is confined to minority neighborhoods, America will continue to turn its back on the problem.

The published government studies do very little to dispel the myths and stereotypes about the Native Americans. What the government should have published are reports that create a more positive image of the Native American. In my opinion, the government studies done on successful Native Americans would have been very appropriate. There is still a need in minority communities for positive role models. A feature story on successful red men and women would be very beneficial to the Native-American community.

In writing about the plight of the Native Americans, I also need to mention the Eskimo Indians of Alaska and Hawaiian Indians of Hawaii, who are also American citizens. What makes these two native tribes different is they live outside the boundaries that make up this country's first 48 states. Although the first Americans to visit Alaska and Hawaii were well aware of the fact they were not in the Indies, they still decided to call the native inhabitants Indians.

Eskimo and Hawaiian tribes suffered the same fate as the mainland Native Americans. The government negotiated and purchased the Alaskan Territory and the Hawaiian Islands. The problem with this is the people the United States negotiated with did not own the land. The natives who were the original occupants of Alaska and Hawaii owned this land but had no say in the sale of their property to the government. The fact that the natives had established possession of this land was never given consideration. Just as they did to the Native Americans, the white man moved to Alaska and Hawaii and took over land that belonged to the natives.

The Eskimos who live in Alaska today are still treated like second-class citizens. Although Eskimos make up a large portion of the population in Alaska, they do not have equal representation in Alaska's government. On the other hand, the Hawaiian tribes are slowly taking control of their native land. Hawaii's government, as well as its economic and social systems, is well represented by native Hawaiians. Where does one find a member of the red race in America today? Some citizens of the United States have not had the privilege of meeting their fellow countrymen, the Native Americans. Contrary to popular belief, all the Native Americans in this country do not live on reservations. Unlike the

45

stereotypes that are common to the Indians, Native Americans become butchers, bakers, and candle stick makers as well as doctors, lawyers and, of course, Native-American chiefs. To answer the question regarding where the Native American can be found in America, just take a good look around because they live in neighborhoods near you and me.

The facts and opinions in this book, regarding how Native Americans have been discriminated against, contain insufficient details and descriptions of the actual experience. As an African American, I am not qualified to expound on racial injustice in America from the perspective of the Native Americans.

It nauseates me each time I read or listen to a self-proclaimed white "expert" explain how a black man or a red man feels about racial discrimination. A doctorate in philosophy does not entitle any white American to define racial discrimination. The only way for the white American to feel the sting of racial injustice is to walk a mile on a hot day in the South as a bare-foot black slave or to walk a mile in the Winter on the Trail of Tears in the moccasins of a Native American. I close this chapter with a sincere apology, because, if any of the facts or opinions contained in this book offend the Native Americans, I am truly sorry. Although I am not qualified to speak on discrimination from the red man's perspective, there is no way I could ever write a book about apartheid in America and not include the Native Americans. I also realize that I only scratched the surface on the subject of American apartheid and the Native Americans. If your appetite calls for more on this subject, I suggest you read a book by a Native American on racial discrimination.

Chapter Three

I t should not take much to make all Americans understand and truly believe that the racial restrictions
in this country are just as bad as the barriers of
apartheid in South Africa. American apartheid is truly a part
of the history of this country. The white race that established
the practice of apartheid in America with its treatment of the
Native American added insult to injury with the enslavement of Africans. Slavery gave the white man the opportunity to practice apartheid at a different level and on a new
victim.

The white man defeated the "Indians," took America
from them and then forced the Native Americans to live on
reservations. African Americans became the second victims
of apartheid when the white man captured their black ancestors in Africa, loaded them on to ships, brought them to
America and then forced the black race to live as slaves on
plantations.

For me, it is a very painful fact that the history of
African Americans in the United States begins with their
enslavement by white Americans. I wish there was a more
attractive way to begin the history of the African-American
culture in this country, but we cannot change the past. We
can only hope for a brighter future.

One of the most difficult tasks a proud African-American father or mother has is teaching the history of the black race to their children. You cannot imagine how difficult it was for me to explain to my young children that the white man once owned their ancestors. Owned, as in the way you own a dog, or the way you own a car, or the way you own any other kind of property.

The difficulty I experienced was not so much in explaining the history of slavery to my children. It was trying to control my anger and teach the facts surrounding slavery at the same time. Whenever I think about the fact that my ancestors were bought and sold like cattle, I lose my temper. It is also very difficult to teach history while trying to hold back tears. Each time I envision the pain and suffering my ancestors endured in slavery, I feel like crying.

The Jews survived the Holocaust, the Native Americans survived the Indian Wars, and the African Americans survived slavery. The three events just mentioned are all race-related tragedies that are products of apartheid, and all but the Holocaust occurred in the United States of America.

The basic concept of slavery is as old as mankind. Slavery played an essential role in the development of the world. Slaves were used as a source of inexpensive labor. Slaves helped build the Roman Empire, the pyramids, the Great Wall of China, and slaves helped build this country. Although the enslavement of Africans in this country was a most evil act, the study of the history of the United States proved it to be a necessary evil. The economic development of all the Southern states depended on agriculture. The sale of crops such as cotton, corn, tobacco and fruit are what helped build the South. The use of black slave labor to harvest those crops and maintain the large plantations on which the crops were grown lessened the expense of production and increased the profits.

As a realist and as a United States citizen, I must agree that slavery was very essential to the development of America. However, as a proud African American, I will never agree that the way my black slave ancestors were treated by their white masters was essential to the development of anything other than a living hell and apartheid. Why were the Africans, who were forced to leave their native land and come to America, treated differently than the white indentured and bond servants who were also forced to leave their homes in the old country and come to the New World? Indentured or bond servants were basically slaves. Was the fact that one race of slave was white and the other black the reason they were treated differently by their white masters?

The documented inhumane treatment of African slaves in America is another case of the white man's ability to justify his behavior toward other human beings by labeling them heathens. The early white settlers labeled all non-white people heathens. The white man seemed to believe they had the God-given right to treat all heathens like animals. The heathen label also eliminated any chance of the white man ever feeling guilty for the inhumane treatment of his fellow human beings. How could white men be so sure that a race of people, whose language they could not understand and whose culture they knew nothing about, did not believe and worship the same God as the white man himself?

Why did white men even attempt to make such a judgment of people of color without first getting to know them? The history of both the Native Americans and the Africans has a well-defined tradition of religious belief. The Native Americans had established a belief in a Supreme Being in North America long before the grandparents of Christopher Columbus were born. It was the deep spiritual conviction inherited from their African ancestors that kept hope alive in the black slaves that they would be delivered from the bonds of slavery.

The white apartheid system in America was responsible for the cruel and unusual punishment of the African slaves. These words, usually associated with criminal injustice in this country, should be the words that come to mind when we think of how African slaves were treated by the white slave owners. The cruelty African Americans suffered at the hands of the white man was both physical, mental and fatal. So cruel was the white man's treatment of black slaves that Africans who refused to eat when they arrived in this country were force-fed with a contraption called a "mouth opener." A "mouth opener" was a metal device that had a spoon on top and a compartment on the bottom, which was filled with hot coals. The Africans on hunger strikes were held down, the hot metal was pressed against their lips, and food was forced in when the slaves opened their mouths to scream.

What a price my ancestors paid for freedom, justice and equality——the freedom of speech, the freedom of the press, the freedom of religion and the freedom to vote. Because of the high price paid by the black slaves—their freedom in America—as black Americans, we must never relinquish any of these hard-earned freedoms. We must also practice and participate in these freedoms, the most important of which is the right to vote.

Americans of all races, colors and creeds have fought and died to be free. Not only did they fight for freedom in the United States but in foreign countries as well. Americans fought to preserve democracy and destroy its enemies wherever and whenever it was necessary. World War I, World War II, Korea, Viet Nam and Desert Storm were all battles fought on foreign soil to preserve democracy.

What is democracy? Democracy is simply the right of the people to choose the way they want to live and be governed. Democracy is merely another word for freedom. In order for a true democracy to exist and be successful, there can be no discrimination for any reason. Each man or woman, regardless of race, color or creed, must have an equal choice and must be free.

The Declaration of Independence, the Constitution and the Bill of Rights, the words in these famous American documents spell out the essence of freedom in this country. "We hold these truths to be self-evident that all men are created equal" and should have equal rights. The quote you just read is at the heart of all those famous American documents. All people—not just all white people, but all people—are created equal and should have equal rights. Why did white Americans lose sight of the goal of every native or foreign-born citizen of this country since Ben Franklin? The goal then and now is life, liberty and the pursuit of happiness. Why did white Americans deny Africans their freedom? The answer is very simple: to preserve the system of apartheid in America.

The enslavement of black men and women was practiced legally in America; yet, the laws of the land clearly intended that all people are created equal. The white men wrote the laws; therefore, the laws only applied to white men. To most of the white people who lived in this country, the laws made good sense. Like the Native Americans before them, the white man never considered Africans to be men; therefore, the white man's laws were not intended for non-white people.

Most African Americans have been offended by racial slurs or stereotypes at some point in their lives. I can remember one incident that hurt me deeply when I was a teenager. I was on a neighborhood baseball team. The baseball teams in my neighborhood had just been integrated, and I was the only black kid on the 14 to 16-year-old team. The fact that I was the only black player on the team never seemed to matter. I knew all the other players because we went to the same high school.

The coach used to pile all 15 of the kids on my team into a few cars whenever we had to travel to play a game. On the ride home from a game one day, a car in front of us suddenly cut us off. I was riding in the back with several of my teammates, and I heard one of the players sitting in the front say, "It must have been a woman driver." We all laughed. As we got closer to the car that had cut us off, I heard that same teammate say, "That's not a woman driver. That's a man." The statement was barely out of his mouth, when the man who was driving the car I was riding in shouted, "That's not a man. That's a nigger."

All my white teammates dropped their heads and turned red as they blushed in embarrassment. For the first time since I had become a member of this team, I felt all alone. I was not angry. I was hurt and disappointed. I thought all these white people liked and respected me. The man driving the car was the older brother of one of my teammates. How could he say something like that while I was in his car? If he felt that way about African Americans, maybe all my teammates felt that way but never said it to my face.

I never went back to play on that team again, even though several of the white kids from the team came to me and apologized for what had been said. It was not the first time I had heard someone called a "nigger" by a white person. When it happened before, I just thought the white person did not like black people. This was the first time I realized that being called a "nigger" by a white man meant being called less than a man or less than a human being.

When the white man stole my ancestors from Africa, he stole their freedom. Freedom is more precious than silver and gold. Freedom is as precious as life itself. According to

ᚱᚱᚱᚱᚱᚱᚱᚱᚱᚱᚱᚱᚱᚱᚱᚱᚱᚱᚱᚱᚱᚱᚱᚱᚱᚱᚱᚱᚱᚱᚱᚱᚱᚱᚱ

the Bible, one of the Ten Commandments states, "Thou shalt not steal." The act of enslavement is a felony listed under the kidnaping statute of the law. The Holocaust was a crime. The treatment of the Native Americans in this country was a crime, and slavery was a crime.

The first African slaves were brought to this country on merchant ships. White merchants sailed to the coast of Africa and traded goods to native African tribes in exchange for a few black captives. The black captives were the spoils of wars between African tribes. The white merchants brought these African slaves to America and sold or traded them to white plantation owners.

The black slaves became a popular item in the South. One of the reasons Africans became so popular as field hands in the South was because they were used to the hot climate. The African slaves had the natural ability to work longer in the heat than the white man. The economic theory of supply and demand left its mark on the progression of slavery in America. With the increase in the demand for African slaves, so came the need for an increase in the supply of blacks in America. The slave trade, the buying and selling of Africans, became big business.

Slave traders would buy ships and enlist men to hunt and capture Africans or trade with African tribes for captive slaves. The slave trade became so lucrative that the West coast of Africa became known as the "Gold Coast," and Africans captured or traded were called "black gold." Now you know the first reference to "black gold" in America was not used to describe oil.

Slave trade became such a large business that ships were built specifically to transport slaves as cargo. Ships were designed with false bottoms so that the slaves could be hidden on board. Some countries outlawed the slave trade, and their naval vessels would capture ships that were carrying slaves as cargo, free the slaves and arrest the ship's crew. To avoid being captured with slaves on board, some captains of ships loaded with slaves would open the false bottom of the ship and let the slaves down into the ocean.

To get an idea of how inhumane it was to ship slaves across the Atlantic Ocean to America, I recommend you look at the diagram of a slave ship. Two excellent examples of slave ship deck plans are the "Plan of the Brookes" found in *From Slavery to Freedom* by John Hope Franklin and the deck plan of a French slave ship found in *An American History* , a book by Rebecca Brooks Gruver. What these diagrams will show is how hundreds of black slaves were packed like sardines in a can. Black slaves had to endure cramped conditions for months as they were shipped from Africa to America.

Just think how terrible the Holocaust had to be for the Jews and how devastating the injustice suffered by the Native Americans had to be, for me to rank slavery as number three on the list of man's worst case of inhumane treatment of his fellow man.

I own a few thoroughbred race horses; therefore, I attend thoroughbred horse auctions, and I have witnessed how prime stock is sold at auction. The horses are paraded around and looked over from head to toe. Some prospective horse buyers feel the thoroughbreds' rumps, legs and even check their teeth. The horses are never referred to by name, only by a number placed on their hips. The auction starts, and the horses are sold to the highest bidder. This was, basically, the same way African slaves were sold at auction.

White slave traders would parade black slaves in front of white plantation owners. The white plantation owners would go through the same routine as a prospective thoroughbred horse buyer. The white plantation owners would feel the arms and legs of the slaves and check their teeth the same as was done to the horses.

Just like the horse auctions, slaves auctions were open to the public. The fact that these auctions were held in a public forum made this undignified pawing by strange white men even more humiliating for the Africans. Unlike the horse auction, the white plantation owners were allowed to take their examination of their potential purchases to another level.

The white plantation owners would physically check the genital area of black male slaves to ensure their ability to reproduce. Young black male slaves, like the thoroughbred horse, increased in value based on their potential as studs. This is the reason African-American males today are very offended when white people call them "stud" or "buck."

The white plantation owners would make a public spectacle of black female slaves by stripping them of what little clothing they had so the white man could physically measure their breast size and pelvic area. The probing hands and eyes of the white slave masters upon the bodies of African female slaves had a two-fold purpose, one of which had nothing to do with assessing the monetary value of the slave. The white man, for the most part, was checking the black female slaves for their breeding potential, which would enhance the value of the African female slave. However, the white plantation owners also had lust in their hearts and on their minds as they gazed at the black female slaves as future sex partners.

Female slaves were used by their white masters as sex partners. Slaves had no choice but to accept the advances of their white masters or be raped and physically abused. Why would the white slave masters find pleasure in having sex with women whom they considered to be heathens? This lust for slave sex partners was not just confined to the white male slave masters. The cultured and refined white women who lived on the Southern plantation took black male slaves as sex partners as well.

If a white female discovered her husband or a male family member was having sex with a black female slave, the white female would either accept the fact that the white male had a black mistress, or the female slave was merely sold to another plantation. The male slave was not as fortunate when a white male caught him having sex with a white woman. The black male slaves were shot or lynched.

When a white woman was caught having sex with a black male slave, she would swear the African slave forced himself on her, which was a crime punishable by death. In the rare cases when the white women confessed that they initiated the sexual relationship with the black male slaves, the white slave master still shot or lynched the black male slaves to protect the honor and innocence of the white female. It was a tradition during the Civil War era, and still practiced today, true Southerners will do anything to protect the honor of aristocratic white women, also known as "Southern belles."

The honor of a Southern white woman was the major issue in the famous court case of the "Scottsboro Boys." As I recall, the case took place in 1931 in Scottsboro, a town in Alabama. In this famous court case, two white women claimed they were raped by several young black men. The fact of the matter was the white women were simply caught in the act of having sex with some black men by a white man. The evidence in this case clearly indicated the white women were lying. Although the white women who accused these black men were of questionable character and lacked acceptable moral fiber, an all-white jury found the black men guilty of rape. The only reason why they were found guilty dates back to the days of slavery. If a white woman swore a black man raped her, the black man was automatically guilty.

Although they were clearly innocent, the young black

men were sentenced to death. Having sex with a white woman was going to cost them their lives.

Once a plantation owner bought a slave, that slave became his property. The fact that slaves were the property of their white masters was the law of the land. Just think, a country that fought the Revolutionary War to gain its freedom from England would allow laws that would make it legal for one race of men to own another race of men.

In order to prove Africans were property and not human beings, some white masters branded their slaves like they branded their horses and cattle. Branding, for those of you who are not familiar with the term, is a permanent identification mark. An animal is branded by taking a red hot metal object and burning a design or initial on the animal's skin. The animal is tied so it cannot move or run away. The animal screams out in pain after the hot iron touches its skin. The white master used the same procedure to brand their slaves. Sometimes, I can still hear the slaves scream in pain from the master's branding iron.

Can you imagine how a red hot piece of metal applied to your skin might feel? Hold a lighted match against your arm for about a second, then multiple that feeling times a thousand. That may give you some idea of how slaves felt after being branded. Just remember a few things while holding that match against your skin. You get to hold the match against your own skin by choice, and you get to remove the match and stop whenever things get too hot. Slaves did not have a choice. Their hands and feet were tied, and they were held down until white masters felt the branding was done.

Because most African slaves were field hands, the white masters saw no need for the slaves to be educated. In some states, it was against the law for a slave to know how to read and write. It was also against the law for anyone, white or black, to teach a slave how to read or write. Why do you think the white masters did not want the African slaves taught to read and write because knowledge is power. Knowledge breeds discontent. Knowledge is contagious, and knowledge is freedom.

The white masters were afraid that an education might restore some of the pride and dignity to the black slaves. Africans who were too proud and dignified to accept slavery were whipped by the white masters until they submitted and finally accepted their slave status. The white man always made it a point to gather all his slaves so they could witness him beating an uncooperative slave. The white master wanted all his slaves to see the pain and suffering, and it was used as a fear tactic to keep them in line.

Some proud Africans were beaten to death because they refused to be slaves. "And before I be a slave, I be lying in my grave. Oh freedom there for me." These are words from a so-called "Negro spiritual"; the point being that some of my African ancestors chose to die rather than be slaves.

The thirst for knowledge inspired some African slaves to learn to read and write. Although it could cost them their lives if the white masters found out black slaves could read, the slaves continued to learn how to read and write. Knowledge is contagious. One slave would learn to read and write and that slave would teach other slaves. This thirst for knowledge was so strong that it caused some slaves to run away in search of a source of knowledge beyond the boundaries of the plantation.

Chapter Four

The beginning of the Civil War may be the first time some history teachers associated freedom with the black man. There were some Africans who managed to gain their freedom in this country long before the Civil War. Freedom came to the Africans in a variety of different ways. Some Africans were just given their freedom by the white plantation owners. Some Africans were able to earn enough money to buy their own freedom from their white owners. Other black slaves ran away from the plantation and never came back. Contrary to popular belief, some Africans did manage to survive in America in an environment other than as a slave living on a plantation.

The Civil War was the culmination of the move to abolish slavery and free the African slaves. However, there was a small group of individuals who fought to end slavery before the Civil War. That group was made up of runaway slaves, free Africans and white Americans who opposed slavery. They created a system that helped the slaves gain their freedom. The group aided in the escape of the slaves from the plantation and provided them with food, shelter and a safe route to Canada and freedom. The system was known as the "Underground Railroad."

As an African American, I would like to thank Canada for providing a safe haven for runaway slaves to begin a new life. The majority of blacks who live in Canada today are direct descendants of slaves who escaped from America to find freedom. The black Canadians should, in turn, thank the African-American descendants of Harriet Tubman, the former slave, who was a famous conductor on the Underground Railroad.

The ability to read and write opened the door for the slaves to obtain a higher education. That door to higher education would eventually lead the slaves to freedom. Education was a bright light that helped the slaves find their lost pride and dignity. By denying slaves the right to an education, the white man kept the black slaves in the dark for a long time.

The issue of Africans being denied the right to obtain an equal education existed in this country during slavery, and it still exists as a major problem today. I will discuss my opinions regarding equal educational opportunities for African Americans later in this book. Just remember, if knowledge is power, the cobblestones of knowledge are used to pave the road to success, and education is the driving force to increase knowledge.

Knowledge can be used to create a powerful positive force for good, but the lack of knowledge can be used just as effectively as a powerful negative force for evil. One of the main reasons Africans remained slaves for as long as they did in this country was their lack of knowledge. Most African slaves were, in fact, ignorant to the ways of white America. They were just as ignorant as any Irish, Polish, Russian, Italian or any other nationality of immigrants when they first came to America. The difference between the Africans who came to America and the other white immigrants was the color of their skins. White immigrants were not sold as slaves, and it was not illegal to teach them how to read and write.

When a police officer stops a motorist for exceeding the posted speed limit, the motorist sometimes tries to explain to the police officer that the reason he is speeding is because he did not see a speed limit sign. The police officer gives the motorist a speeding ticket and drives away. Is the motorist guilty of breaking the law? The motorist takes the ticket to traffic court to let a judge decide if he or she actually broke the law. In court, when the judge asks the motorist why he or she was speeding, the motorist states he or she never saw a speed limit sign. The judge's response is that ignorance is no excuse for not obeying the law, and the judge finds the motorist guilty.

The point of this story? Does the fact that the slaves were ignorant give them an excuse for remaining slaves in this country for nearly 250 years? Is there a difference in the ignorance of the motorist for not knowing the speed limit and the ignorance of the slaves? I place no blame on the African slaves for their ignorance, for there can be no blame for being ignorant of the light when you are forced to live in darkness.

When a motorist signs a driver's license, that license gives the motorist the privilege of operating a motor vehicle on public highways. It is a privilege and not a right. In order to maintain that privilege, the motorist must agree to obey all motor vehicle laws. The rights given to all American citizens are guaranteed in this country. The privileges we have, however, are earned and are not guaranteed. A driver's license comes with a choice. One can choose to drive or not to drive. It is the responsibility of the motorist who chooses to drive to seek out, study and know the motor vehicle laws in order to maintain the privilege of operating a motor vehicle on the highways.

Slavery was neither a privilege agreed to by the Africans nor was it the right of the white man to make the black man slaves. Africans certainly did not become slaves in this country by choice, and they had no choice in the fact that they were totally ignorant of the ways of the white man in America. It was the design of their white masters to keep the slaves as ignorant as possible. It was easy for the white man to maintain his control over the slaves as long as the slaves remained ignorant.

Not only did the white man physically control the slaves, but they also controlled their minds. The white man was able to control the minds of the slaves when they first brought them to this country because the white man was the black slave's only source of knowledge. Control any animal's source of knowledge, and you control that animal's mind as well. This formula will work on all animals including the human.

The minds of the slaves were conditioned by their white masters much like Pavlov's dog. Dr. Pavlov, a famous psychologist, as part of a mind-conditioning experiment, rang a bell each time he fed his dog. After a time, his dog would start to salivate every time he heard a bell, even though he was not fed. In the dog's mind, the sound of the bell was associated with the taste of food. Slave masters would condition the minds of their slaves in much the same way as Pavlov conditioned the mind of his dog.

The slaves were told by their masters, if they ran away from the plantation, they would disappear or be destroyed by evil spirits. When a runaway slave was never heard from again, the master told the remaining slaves that the runaway slave disappeared off the face of the earth. Some runaway slaves were caught and killed by white men in hoods who looked like ghosts. The master would tell his slaves the runaway was killed by evil spirits. Runaway slaves who were returned to the plantation told tales of how these ghosts caught them and whipped them for being a bad runaway slave.

At one point in time, the majority of slaves believed anything and everything they were told by their white owners. Unfortunately, there are a large number of African Americans today who still believe anything and everything a white person says is true. Although they were physically and mentally abused by their white masters, most slaves trusted them. The overwhelming trust of the white man is another problem that still exists today in most black communities. Why is it that in areas of this country which have a black majority population, blacks will choose a white person to represent them in local or federal government rather than elect an African American? In my opinion, this can only be attributed to the old slave mentality.

The reason African slaves trusted their white masters, in spite of all the abuse they endured, was because they had no one else to turn to. Without their white masters, the slaves were lost in America. The white masters provided the slaves with their food, clothing and shelter. The once proud and free Africans had very little choice but to form a bond with the provider of their basic needs. By providing the slaves with these basic needs, the white masters had another means of controlling the slaves. Some slaves became so attached to their white masters that they refused to accept freedom.

The battered spouse syndrome, child abuse and the sexual molestation of children are very sensitive issues today in our nation's social structure. Why does a husband or a wife remain in a home when they are being battered by his or her spouse? Why does one parent allow his or her children to be abused and sexually molested by the other parent? Have abuse victims taken on a slave mentality?

A low self-esteem has been noted as a common trait of adult and child abuse victims. A low-self esteem is the reason abuse victims allow the same person, usually a family member, to abuse him or her time and time again. A member of a dysfunctional family tolerates abuse because he or she depends on the support of the family to supply all basic needs. Most abuse victims lack the courage to go out on their own and start a new life. The white slave owners stripped the slaves of their self-esteem; therefore, most slaves lacked the courage to run away from their abusive white masters. For the slave, much like the abuse victim, the fear of the unknown was far greater than the fear of their master's whip.

There are a number of studies conducted each year in this country in an attempt to determine why husbands and wives are battered and why children become the victims of abuse and sexual molestation. The result of these studies may provide some answers as to why this criminal behavior takes place, and these same studies may also give a basic profile of the people who are most likely to batter their spouse, physically abuse or sexually molest a child. What the studies do not do is offer any acceptable excuse that would justify this deviant behavior. The battered spouse, the abused child and the sexually-molested child are a victim of the same circumstances today that plagued the slaves nearly 400 years ago. Just think, slaves were battered, physically abused and sexually molested, and some white Americans found this behavior by white slave owners to be totally acceptable.

The descriptive details of a battered spouse, an abused child or a sexually molested child will usually make the average American vomit. The descriptive details of the abuse endured by slaves at the hands of their white masters will invoke the anger of most African Americans, but does it have the same emotional impact among white Americans?

Most white historians point to the issue of slavery as the main reason this country fought the Civil War. Those same white historians credit President Abraham Lincoln with ending slavery and giving the black man his freedom in

America. Do you actually believe that the white American citizens of the North declared war on the white American citizens of the South just to free the black man? The enslavement of Africans began over 200 years before the Civil War. It is a recorded fact that slaves fought against the British in this country's Revolutionary War. If the issue of slavery made white Northerners angry enough to fight a war, why did it take them over 200 years to get that angry?

Abraham Lincoln was the 16th president. Was he the first president to consider Africans as people and not property? Was he the first president to actually believe that, "All men are created equal...."? Were the 15 presidents who held the office before Lincoln all bigots? Should all the monuments in this country that honor both President George Washington and President Thomas Jefferson be torn down because they owned slaves? In my opinion, if white historians really believed slavery was a major issue in the Civil War, some of the questions I just raised would have already been answered.

President Lincoln will always be remembered for the Civil War, the Gettysburg Address and the Emancipation Proclamation. Most historians credit Lincoln with freeing the slaves. It is a little known fact, but true, that President Lincoln, during his negotiations with the Confederate states prior to the Civil War, agreed to allow slavery as long as the Confederate states agreed not to secede from the Union. President Lincoln may have been opposed to slavery in America, but he was more concerned with the preservation of the Union and avoiding war. If the Confederate states would have agreed to Mr. Lincoln's proposal, Africans may still have been slaves today.

If you count all the casualties from all the wars this country has fought, more white American soldiers were killed or wounded during the Civil War than in all the other wars combined. Not only did the Civil War divide the United States, in some cases, the issues surrounding the Civil War divided families. The war was noted for having brothers, as well as fathers and sons, fight on opposite sides. Northerners who never owned slaves fought for the Confederate army, and former Southern slave owners fought for the Union army.

As an afterthought from earlier chapters of this book, which were written about the Native Americans, historians recorded the War Between the States as this country's only civil war. It was called the Civil War because it was fought exclusively in the United States, and all the participants in this war were Americans. The dictionary defines a civil war as "a war between geographical sections or political factions of the same nation." According to this definition, all the wars between the Native Americans and the white Americans in this country should have been called civil wars. Just something to think about.

Chapter Five

The major concern, as well as the reason this country fought a civil war, was an old issue that just resurfaced. That issue was taxation without representation. The 13 colonies declared their independence from England and fought the Revolutionary War over the issue of taxation without representation. For these same basic reasons, the South seceded from the United States and formed the Confederate States of America. Southerners felt they did not have equal representation in Congress. They also felt that the people who lived in the Southern states were being taxed unfairly, and their tax money was being used to finance the building of Northern industry.

Although it is my opinion that the Civil War was not fought because of the issue of slavery, I do feel that slavery did play a major role in the Union's victory over the Confederacy. The abolition of slavery was used by the Union as a weapon to defeat the South. The Union strategy was to destroy the main source of revenue in the South, and the Confederacy would be destroyed.

The cotton industry was the core of the South's economic system and the main source of revenue for the Confederacy. The slaves were the backbone of the cotton industry because they provided the primary source of labor. The

Union realized very early in the war, if it could destroy the cotton industry in the South, the Confederacy would eventually collapse. The abolition of slavery meant the destruction of the cotton business and the end of the Confederate States of America.

After the U.S. government abolished slavery, it was illegal for anyone to own slaves in this country. In many cases, Union troops were sent to the South to enforce that new law and free slaves. Most slaves welcomed their long-awaited freedom with open arms, while other slaves had to be forced to leave the plantation. Union soldiers had to literally carry some blacks from their former slave quarters. Kicking and screaming as they were being dragged away, the newly freed black Americans shouted at the Union troops that they did not want to leave their white masters, and they did not want to leave their homes.

Social workers today, who go into a home to remove an abused child, face the same resistance from that child as the Union soldiers encountered from some former black slaves. Some abused children think being battered by their parents is a normal way of life. These abused children scream and holler, and the social workers usually have to physically remove them from their homes. Why would children want to stay in homes where they are continually abused by their parents? Because it is the only home they have ever had.

By the time slavery was abolished in America, there were ninth and tenth generations of slaves born in this country. There were very few Africans alive in America who could actually remember what it really felt like to be born free. Although the stories of life in Africa were passed along from one generation of slaves to another, it was hard to keep the hope of freedom strong in all slaves. For some slaves, the plantation was the only home they ever had, and, like the abused child, they did not want to leave.

Thousands of freed slaves joined the Union army and fought against the Confederate troops. The historical accounts of African Americans who actually fought and died in the Civil War were hard to find when I was growing up. I am very glad that the black children of today are able to see movies and read books that feature the details of the African-American soldiers in the Civil War.

The Union also used the abolition of slavery as a weapon for psychological warfare to defeat the Confederacy. The Union strategy was to mix slavery and religion to make abolition a strong moral issue. Supporters of the Union used a classic story from the Bible to portray the abolition of slavery as the struggle of good versus evil. The Union wanted to abolish slavery and free the black man; therefore, the Union was on the side of good. On the other hand, the Confederate States of America wanted to continue slavery, so this put it on the side of evil.

Not all of America took part in the War Between the States. There were several states and territories in this country that decided not to participate in the Civil War, and they remained neutral. Supporters of the Union used the abolition of slavery as a moral deterrent to prevent the neutral states and territories from joining or supporting the Confederacy.

The abolition of slavery caused the destruction of the cotton industry in the South and made it difficult for the Confederacy to solicit financial support from any of the neutral states or territories. Without money for food or equipment, the Confederate army was weakened; thus, making it possible for the Union army to defeat them and bring the war to an end.

In America today, the subject of slavery is seldom discussed in the white community. On the rare occasion when it is discussed, there is very little mention of the abuse suffered by the black slaves. Most white Americans fail to realize that the abuse of slaves, which happened over one 100 years ago, still has a strong influence on the people who live in both the white and black neighborhoods in America today.

Studies have shown that children from dysfunctional families grow up to be dysfunctional adults. The African ancestors of black Americans were forced by the white man to live in a dysfunctional environment called slavery. Most of the dysfunctional behavior of some African Americans today can be traced back to slavery.

Nearly 250 years of slavery, more than 10 generations, dismantled the structure of the family unit for some Africans in this country. The concept of family was non-existent for some ninth and tenth generations of slaves. Just as some ninth and tenth generation of slaves never knew what it felt like to be born free, some also never experienced the togetherness of a family unit.

Slavery was a business, and slaves were property. Because they were property, African slaves who were blood relatives could be sold to another plantation and never see each other again. Children were taken from their mothers and sold. Brothers and sisters were separated and sold. Most of us know what it feels like to have a family member move away from home. However, in most cases, the family members keep in touch and visit each other. Just think how you would feel if someone came into your home, took your children or your mother or father, and told you that you would never see them again.

Slave mothers would cry and suffer the pain of losing a child, but once the white master decided to take the child, there was nothing the slave mother could do to stop it. Some black mothers killed their children at birth rather than have them born slaves or face the possibility of them being sold by their white masters. After a time, slave mothers refused to become emotionally attached to their babies. There is no greater love than that of a mother for her child. The enslavement of the African Americans in this country may not have destroyed that love, but it caused it to be permanently scarred.

Because of what slavery did to the mothers of my African ancestors, I have no choice but to rank the enslavement of black people in America as tied for second on my list of man's greatest inhumanity toward man.

The white slave owners felt the slaves were animals, and, therefore, incapable of having human emotions. The slave owners used the young male slaves to breed with female slaves. Slaves had no choice in the selection of their mates, and the only purpose of the union was to produce new slaves. The minds of the young male slaves were conditioned by the slave owners to believe they were "studs" and not fathers. Slave owners conditioned young female slaves to have sex with whomever the masters selected. Once the female slave was pregnant, the breeding process was completed. The master would then mate another female slave with his young male "buck."

Some white plantation owners made more money selling slaves than they did selling cotton. This made the mating of slaves even more important and the demand to produce slaves even greater. Because of the increased demand for slaves, the white slave owners forced the black slaves to commit incest. Fathers were forced to mate with their daughters, brothers with sisters and mothers with their own sons. When the slave owner ordered a slave couple to mate, to make sure the slaves were actually mating, the master would watch.

Watching slaves have sex both entertained and sexually aroused their masters. Some white plantation owners were so entertained that they often invited friends to watch

71

their slaves having sex. Not only did slave masters force the young female slaves to have sex with young male slaves, they were also forced to have sex with the slave owners and their friends.

The slave masters habitually raped and sexually molested their young female slaves. Having sex with their female slaves became so routine that the slave masters demanded that their young female slaves remain virgins. This assured the slave owners of being the first man to have sex with the female slave. Another reason female slaves had to remain virgins was to assure the master that she had not had sex with a male slave. No self-respecting white man could ever have sex with a woman who had slept with a black man.

Prior to the Civil War, there were approximately four million slaves in America. Of those four million slaves, 400,000 had white fathers. These numbers are just to give you an idea of how many children resulted from sexual encounters between the black female slaves and their white masters. In the 1700's, the law in most states in this country maintained that if a person were of black parents or grandparents, they, too, were black. Therefore, these sons and daughters from mixed parents became slaves. I hope that it will not shock you to know that this law is still on the books in the majority of the states in America.

As a man, when I think about a woman being raped, I envision myself being forcibly sodomized as a way to compare the ordeal of being raped. Just the thought of being a rape victim makes me sick to my stomach. Male slaves did not escape the wrath of the white slave master's sexual abuse. Although the slave owners treated most young male slaves like prized thoroughbred stallions, they also suffered the same sexual defamation that is common to the thoroughbred horse. Like some young thoroughbred horses that are too high-spirited to train, some young black male slaves, whom the white masters found hard to control, were gelded.

For those of you who are not familiar with the term "gelded," it is a surgical procedure performed to remove a male animal's testicles. Gelding an animal is supposed to make him gentle; gelding a black slave was supposed to make him easier for the white man to control. If, after being gelded the black male slave continued to be a problem, the white slave master had the black male slave castrated. "Castration" is a surgical procedure performed to cut off a male animal's penis. I cannot begin to imagine how this affected the black male slaves, but, if it happened to me, I would feel like a part of me had been destroyed, and it would be very difficult for me to ever feel whole again.

The rape and sexual molestation of the black female slaves by white men were brutal crimes. Sexual molestation and rape are both felonies, and, in most states in this country, anyone found guilty of committing these crimes would wind up with a life sentence in prison. Yet, white men raped and molested my ancestors, and it was considered acceptable behavior. Why were these inhumane sex crimes tolerated in a so-called morally-conscious society?

Because the white men owned the slaves, it was okay for the white masters to cut off the genitals of black male slaves, invade the bodies of innocent black female slaves and molest black slave children. These same crimes committed by black men against white men, women or white children meant instant death. It has only been about 40 years ago that black men accused of raping a white woman or sexually molesting a white child were taken from jails and lynched before they ever had a chance to stand trial. The lynching of black men will be discussed later in this book.

Being raped, sexually mutilated and sexually molested ruined any chance of the black female or male slaves ever having a normal sex life. After being raped, sexually mutilated and sexually molested, I can only imagine that it would be very difficult for a woman or man, black or white, to enjoy the warmth and tenderness of foreplay, the thrill of reaching an emotional climax, or the satisfaction of an orgasm.

The sensation of spontaneous male and female bonding, love, marriage and the joys of parenthood are all experiences that all races of Americans take for granted in this country. From the earliest slave times, the black race was denied the right to experience these feelings in America. After nearly 250 years of slavery, African Americans had to learn how to live again as a family.

What are the remaining psychological effects of slavery on today's African Americans as individuals, as family members, and as members of society in America? For an in-depth answer to this question, I would need to write another book. However, I will take this opportunity to give you just a few of my opinions on this subject.

To me, the high rate of infidelity in some African American marriages today can be linked to the slave mentality. After hundreds of years of being conditioned by the white man to have multiple sex partners, some black men and women find it difficult to maintain a monogamous relationship. The subsequent results of this behavior is that some black couples in America shy away from marriage and commitment. This behavior also led to an increased number of black marriages ending in divorce.

"The Color Purple" is a book written about African-American culture in the early 1900's. The book was made into a movie by Steven Spielberg, one of Hollywood's most famous producers and directors. The book and movie are fictional accounts of how a black female survived growing up in a dysfunctional African-American family. Although some African Americans were offended by the way the black male

74

and black family were portrayed in the book and in the movie, I personally feel it is one of the best books I have ever read and one of the best movies I have ever seen.

I recommend this book and movie for all young African Americans who are not aware of some of the after-effects of slavery. Some black people cannot stand to hear the ugly truth about their ancestors. However, based on the facts that have been passed on to me from my grandparents, "The Color Purple" is an accurate and truthful account of the events of the past. The book won a Pulitzer Prize, and the movie was nominated for 11 Academy Awards. Not only were the book and movie very enlightening for me, the movie featured nearly an all African-American cast. It is very rare to see so many black movie stars in one production.

The same way that all Africans brought to this country did not accept slavery and were always seeking the opportunity to gain their freedom from the white man, not all African Americans today suffer the negative effects of the enslavement of their ancestors in America. It is very important for you to remember that all the opinions in this book do not apply to all African Americans. In fact, most black Americans, as well as black American families, lead normal, happy and productive lives, in spite of the abuse endured by Africans as a result of slavery.

After all these years, you might think African Americans would forget the fact that the white man raped and sexually molested the women and children of their black ancestors. The evidence left from these crimes were the babies of slave mothers and white slave owner fathers. The problem with trying to forget these crimes of the past is that most African Americans witness the results of the white man raping their ancestors each time they look in a mirror and see the color of their faces. Thanks to the white man, the skin colors of the black Americans in this country, unlike their

African ancestors, are not black.

The complexions of African Americans today come in a variety of colors, from the purest, darkest brown or black, to the lightest of brown or white. The "Godfather of Soul Music," James Brown, sang, "Say it loud. I'm black and I'm proud." It is hard for African Americans to say I am black and proud when they are actually light brown. All proud black Americans would like to be able to trace their roots back to their African ancestors without having to include the invasion of a white trespasser.

The lack of adhesiveness in some African-American families and African-American communities can be directly attributed to skin tone. Some members of African-American families and communities discriminate against other members of their family or community based on their skin complexion. Some light-skinned African Americans will only associate with other light-skinned African Americans because they feel they are close to being white, and, therefore, more intelligent and overall superior to the darker complected black Americans. On the other hand, some light-skinned African Americans will only associate with dark-complected African Americans because they are ashamed of their white blood and want to reassure themselves of their black pride.

Dark-complected African Americans have the same hangups. The darker African Americans choose to associate with other dark African Americans because they dislike and distrust white people, and some dark African Americans associate with lighter African Americans because they prefer white people to black people. The fact that African Americans discriminate against one another because one may be lighter or darker would almost be humorous if not for the fact that it is a serious character flaw.

Not only are African Americans in this country separated by skin complexion, there are also social class barriers that keep blacks apart in this country. Upper-class blacks do not want to live near or associate with lower-class blacks. Middle-class African Americans usually fall somewhere between the two and really do not associate with the upper or the lower-class blacks.

This same social class discrimination concept prolonged the slaves' efforts to unite and defeat the bonds of slavery. The slaves who were allowed to work in the "Big House" or the mansion thought they were better than the slaves who worked in the field. This is the origin of the old slave labels "house niggers" who were better than the "field niggers." Unfortunately, the white man considered them both to be property and both to be less than human. As ignorant and counter-productive as it was for slaves to discriminate against one another, it is just as ignorant and even more counter-productive for today's African Americans to discriminate against each other regardless of the reason.

As an African American, I never want the black Americans in this country to forget slavery. African Americans in this country should continue to pass on the details of why their ancestors were slaves and how African slaves were abused for over 10 generations by the white men in America. These facts surrounding slavery must be passed down from one generation of African American to another in order to preserve our American heritage and our culture.

African Americans should not dwell on the horrors of slavery or use slavery as an excuse to hate the white man. The black man should use the memories of slavery as the Jews have used the memories of the Holocaust. It serves as a permanent reminder to the world of the horrors of racial injustice. Slavery should remind all African Americans of racial injustice as well as the price their ancestors paid for freedom.

Chapter Six

For those African Americans who have a hard time dealing with the subject of slavery, I suggest you read Alex Haley's book, *Roots*, or rent the movie from your local video store. Alex Haley traced his family tree from Africa, through slavery and until today. The book won a Pulitzer Prize, and the made-for-television movies, "Roots" and "Roots, the Next Generation," won several Emmys. There is a theme in "Roots" that all African Americans should remember. "It's hard to know where you're going, if you don't know where you've been."

African Americans should also remember that the beauty of our culture is inherited from our slave ancestors. We owe our love for music, dance and our spirituality to our African ancestors. We are the American sons and daughters of former slaves, but we are also the African sons and daughters of kings and queens. Black Americans must always be just as proud of their heritage as any other ethnic group in America.

The Holocaust will always be remembered as a crime committed against the Jews. I just hope that the world will someday recognize that slavery in America was a crime committed against the black race. Most importantly, we should all hope that tragedies such as the Holocaust, apartheid in South Africa, the destruction of the Native Americans and slavery, never happen again. Never!

In order for African Americans to win the war for racial equality, we must first unite as a people. In order for us to unite, we must remove all the negative scars of slavery that cause us to fight among ourselves. African Americans must realize that the chains of slavery only exist in our minds. We are free at last. In the words of Dr. King, "Free at last! Free at last. Thank God Almighty, we are free at last."

Chapter Seven

Among early rights movements, the Equal Rights Movement, which was the forerunner of the Civil Rights Movement, actually began in America when the first African brought to this country by the white slave traders, refused to be a slave and demanded that the white man set him free and return him to Africa. Unfortunately, the white man did not honor the demands of the African; therefore, it was the first time that a black man was denied his equal rights in America.

If the white man had adhered to the demands of the African and given him his freedom, the history of this country would have been rewritten. Who knows, the Africans may have all decided to go back to Africa, and there would have been no foundation for the African-American culture in America. Since I have already agreed earlier in this book that slavery was necessary to the development and progress of the United States, it would appear that it was also necessary for the black man to be denied the right to be equal to the white man in America.

The Revolutionary War, which started in 1775, the Declaration of Independence, signed in 1776, and the Constitution, enacted in 1789, were all historical events that gave Americans freedom and equal rights. Since slavery predated these celebrated events in American history, it makes the denial of equal rights of the first Africans brought to this country, who were made slaves, a contradiction to the beliefs outlined in the aforementioned documents. It also cheapened the victory of the Revolutionary War because the quality of life did not change for the minority races, Native Americans and African Americans after the war. It would have to be a non-issue because life did not change much for the minority races after these prominent events.

This country's declaration of independence from England, the end of the Revolutionary War and the enactment of the Constitution failed to put an end to racial discrimination. The same events in history that gave freedom to the white man also failed to free the Africans and put an end to slavery. How could white Americans be so blind as to not see slavery as denying the very freedom they wanted from England? Apartheid continued to be the law of the land in America.

The rights of all American citizens are guaranteed and protected by the Constitution. The fact that African Americans and Native Americans fought and died in the Revolutionary War, the same as white Americans, should have earned them the same rights to freedom and equality. It is a well-known fact that the first American to be killed in battle in the Revolutionary War was a runaway slave named Crispus Attucks. Black soldiers distinguished themselves in the Continental Army at the battle of Bunker Hill and other famous military encounters during the Revolutionary War.

Prince Hall was another black American who was very active in America's fight for independence. However, Prince Hall's greatest contribution to African-American history was forming the first African American Masonic Order. Founded in 1784, the Prince Hall order is the largest black fraternal organization in America today. What makes the creation of this organization such a monumental event in history and the group so special is the fact that the Prince Hall Masons were the first African-American male group to bond together in an effort to improve conditions for blacks in America. They were also the first black American organization that publicly exhibited a pride in the African heritage. I am extremely proud to be a member of the Landmark No. 40, Free and Accepted Masonic Prince Hall Lodge.

Those of you who belong to fraternal organizations may want to find out more about Prince Hall, the Revolutionary War hero. This is not a history book. I do suggest you check the library for the names of some other black Revolutionary War heroes such as Peter Salem, Salem Poor, Pomp Blackman and Barzillai Lew. You just might be surprised at what you will find, and, if not surprised, at least you will have some very interesting material to read.

After serving so valiantly in the Revolutionary War, you would think that the white Continental Army soldiers would have invited the African slaves and the Native Americans to their "victory party." Rather than receiving decorations for their accomplishments, after the Revolutionary War, General George Washington issued an order to all of his commanding officers directing that blacks were no longer needed to fight in the military, and, therefore, African Americans would no longer be enlisted in the army. Shortly after General Washington issued that order, the Continental Congress made it a law that "Negroes" could not serve in the army. This law was the first time that white America cast the black soldier aside after a war was over. Unfortunately, this trend would continue.

If only white Americans had the vision to include the Africans and the Native Americans in their celebration of independence, I am sure the Native Americans and African Americans would have welcomed the invitation and joined the freedom jubilee. Why is it always possible for black, red and white men to stand together, to fight and to die in war, yet find it impossible to live together in peace? Most white Americans lack the courage to face the reality of being equal to the Africans and Native Americans. White men are quick to forget that the same black soldiers and red soldiers they befriended and trusted in war are the same black men and red men they discriminated against in peace.

It would appear that the white man's desire to maintain a system of apartheid is stronger than the bonds of trust and friendship men develop during a war. American apartheid and white supremacy go hand in hand. Without this system of apartheid in America, the white race would lose power, and, if the white race lost power, it would lose control of America. This may be the first time you see the words American apartheid and white supremacy used in the same sentence. The two views are synonymous and equally disgusting. I take this opportunity to warn you I will continue to associate these two disgusting concepts throughout this book.

Although today's African Americans have not achieved total equality, we have come a mighty long way since the days of slavery. The war to defeat racial discrimination and put an end to the problems associated with American apartheid are ongoing battles for the minority races. The progress made to establish total racial equality and end racial discrimination can be attributed to the courage and the determination of the civil rights workers in America.

The history of the civil rights workers can be traced to the first runaway slaves who managed to escape to freedom. It was from this group of runaway slaves that the first Freedom Fighters were born. They were called Freedom Fighters because they were fighting to free slaves. These runaway slaves, assisted by white Americans who opposed

83

slavery, joined together to help slaves who had run away from the plantation. The group developed a plan that guided the runaway slaves along their journey to freedom. The system was known as the "Underground Railroad."

One reason it was called the "Underground Railroad" was because the people who helped the runaway slaves conducted an extremely covert operation. It had to be a highly secret operation because it was against the law for slaves to run away from their white owners, and it was against the law for anyone to aid or assist a runaway slave. In some Southern states, members of the "Underground Railroad" actually risked their lives in an effort to free slaves because the punishment for the crime of aiding or harboring a slave was death by hanging.

It was impossible for the Freedom Fighters to transport runaway slaves or to travel on any of the main roads during the daytime. Because it was so very dangerous to give aid to runaway slaves, it was necessary for the Freedom Fighters to establish several indirect routes to transport runaway slaves from the South to the North. In order to make the trip to freedom as safe as possible for the runaway slaves, the Freedom Fighters set up shelters along the way so the runaway slaves could rest during the day and move on after it was dark.

The Freedom Fighters who operated these shelters were white Americans and free African slaves who lived in the Northern states and Western territories and opposed slavery. Prior to the Civil War, this small group of white Freedom Fighters and "non-slaves" would be joined in their battle to end slavery by other white Americans who also opposed slavery. These white Americans were known as abolitionists.

Runaway slaves were provided with food, clothing and a "Freedom Fighter" to guide them to the next shelter.

The increasing number of runaway slaves created what appeared to be a revolving door as they moved in and out of each shelter. The increased activity at the shelters resembled the commotion at a railroad station, which was another reason why this covert operation was called the "Underground Railroad."

Most of the credit for the success of the "Underground Railroad," which helped runaway slaves escape to Canada and freedom, belongs to a runaway slave named Harriet Tubman. She was born a second-generation black slave on a plantation in Virginia. Her courage and determination made it possible for her to overcome the handicap of being both black and a slave to become an African-American heroine.

Harriet Tubman ran away from her plantation and found her way to freedom in the North. She was not content with having gained her own freedom, returning to plantations in the South to help other slaves run away. Time and time again, at the risk of her own freedom, Harriet used the Underground Railroad to lead hundreds of slaves to freedom. History records that on several of her trips into the South, she was captured by white slave traders and returned to a life of slavery. However, each time she was captured, she managed to escape and return to the fight for freedom and the battle to end slavery in America.

There have been several books written about the life of Harriet Tubman. I even remember a made-for-television movie that featured her autobiography. I feel personally indebted to Harriet Tubman for what she did for my African-American ancestors, and I strongly suggest that you visit your local library and read her autobiography. I think it would be a benefit to all the citizens of this country to study and learn from the example set by this great American.

It would be an act of total negligence if I did not

highlight the efforts of the early white American "Freedom Fighters." Whereas there have been several books written about the black Freedom Fighter Harriet Tubman, there is documentation available that chronicles the efforts of the early white American Freedom Fighters. Most books that are available barely mention that the majority of the white American Freedom Fighters were Quakers, a religious group mainly located in Pennsylvania. The Quakers played a very active role in the Underground Railroad.

It was the Quakers who guided the runaways through the North, and it was the Quakers who used their homes as the shelters for runaway slaves as they moved north to Canada. Quakers have always been well known for their strong religious conviction and their beliefs regarding non-violence. Although Quakers are conscientious objectors to war and refuse to become active members of the armed forces, they have risked their lives on the battlefield fighting for the freedom of the slaves.

In all the wars that Americans have participated, Quakers have been there on the front, delivering supplies to the troops or rendering aid to the wounded. Quakers are quiet people who choose not to lead a very active social life. Because of their quiet persona, Quakers generally do not seek or receive a great deal of publicity. Maybe after people read this book, the Quakers will receive even more of the credit they deserve for their role as early civil rights workers.

As an African American, I feel we should have a greater awareness of the white Americans who were always opposed to slavery in America. I think black Americans should seek out and study any documentation that pertains to the early white American freedom fighters. We should pass this information along to our children and encourage them to study it and pass it on to their children. African Americans need to realize that white Americans fought and died in an effort to gain freedom and equal rights for their ancestors long before the Civil War.

Unfortunately, there are some black Americans today who still follow an old tradition of being treated the same as the Africans were during slavery, and just as unfortunate, there are still some white Americans who still suffer from the same hatred and bigotry that condoned the practice of slavery, white supremacy and apartheid. Just as African Americans follow in the footsteps of their ancestors and continue the battle for equality in America, there are white Americans who maintain the family tradition of fighting to end racial discrimination. Although the modern white civil rights workers have faced their share of trials and tribulations, they did not face the automatic death sentence that their white ancestors faced for being freedom fighters.

Prior to the Civil War, a group of runaway slaves formed an army in the South with the purpose of fighting to end slavery. This army raided white plantations throughout the South and freed slaves. These raids resulted in violent confrontations between the white residents of these plantations and the slave army. With each assault on a Southern plantation, the size of the slave army increased. Liberated slaves joined the slave army and became soldiers in the battle to end slavery in the South.

The most noted of these raids by the slave army on Southern white plantations were led by a slave named Nat Turner. Under his leadership, a small group of runaway slaves was responsible for killing about 60 white Virginians. White historians characterize Nat Turner as being a "fanatic," a "maniac," "fiend-like" and "perverted." The other members of his slave army were described as "marauders" because of their acts of violence committed against the white Virginians.

It is strange how American history glorifies the white

men who fought to win their freedom by calling them "revolutionists." When a white "revolutionist" killed an Englishman in an attempt to gain his freedom, he was a hero. George Washington, the leader of the revolutionary army, became the "father" of our country. On the other hand, a runaway slave who fought the white slave owners to gain his freedom was called a "terrorist," and, if he killed a white man, it was called murder. Washington became the nation's first president, and Nat Turner, the leader of the slave revolt, was captured by the white Southern militia and hanged.

What do Daniel Boone, General George Armstrong Custer and Buffalo Bill Cody have in common? They are all white American heroes who earned their fame by killing Native Americans. They are all American legends who have been immortalized in books and movies. Nat Turner was an African-American hero. He should have received as much positive notoriety in American history as the aforementioned white American heroes.

Nat Turner was a martyr. He lost his life while fighting to free his people. Why, then, is his name not a household word in America? How come we never see a postage stamp to commemorate the memory of Nat Turner? Why is it that black Americans are unable to go to the video store and rent a movie on the exploits of this African-American hero? Do white Americans still fear the memory of Nat Turner?

He killed white people in a country that practices apartheid. There is no way that American history could make this "murderer" of so-called innocent white slave masters a positive role model. He was an inspiration to the downtrodden masses of slaves everywhere. He inspired them to rise up and fight the white man for their freedom. The idea of blacks killing whites to achieve freedom in the late 1800's and equality was horrifying for white Americans. I can imagine the thought of a Nat Turner resurfacing today must be just as horrifying.

In another contrast of this same scenario, we have the adventures of John Brown, a famous white abolitionist. He was also labeled a "fanatic" and a "terrorist" by most white historians in America, and he did almost the same things as Nat Turner. Brown organized a gang of white anti-slave supporters and runaway slaves, and they raided plantations in the South to free slaves. His army also grew in size after each successful assault. His most famous raid happened in 1859 when he led his troops in an attack on an arsenal in Harpers Ferry, West Virginia. During his so-called reign of terror in the South, Brown's army killed over 100 white supporters of slavery.

He, like Nat Turner, was caught and hanged. Unlike Nat Turner, however, Brown became a martyr for the abolition and a legendary American folk hero. Both Turner and Brown fought and killed white people in the battle to end slavery. Turner was labeled a murderer, and Brown became a hero. The only difference in these two men, both great Americans heroes, is the color of their skin. One was white, and the other was black.

The white mentality regarding these two men is the same today. It was all right for runaway slaves to kill white people as long as they were led by a white man, but it was totally unacceptable if they were led by a black man. How does this compare to the white man's thinking of today? Just look at   sports. The white team owners in football and baseball are more than happy to let black athletes star in a supporting role with white players, but these same white owners will never vote to allow an African American to become commissioner of a league or vote to allow African Americans to own their own team.

Today, white America is moderately tolerant of the non-violent Civil Rights Movement; therefore, this non-violent movement has became tortoise-like in its ability to advance the cause of racial equality. Although I do not advocate violence as a means to end racial discrimination, I do feel, however, that the black civil rights leaders of today could use a little of Nat Turner's mentality as they plan the battles in the war to gain racial equality in America.

The slaves who found their road to freedom with the help of the Underground Railroad escaped into Canada where slavery was illegal. Africans who escaped slavery and found freedom in Canada were usually from Maryland, Delaware, Virginia, Kentucky, Tennessee and North Carolina. These slave states were close enough to the Northern border for the Underground Railroad to smuggle effectively runaway slaves into Canada.

Some runaway slaves from the Southern-most slave states such as Arkansas, Mississippi, Georgia, South Carolina and Florida escaped to freedom by crossing the Florida border into Spanish territory or crossing the Texas territorial border into Mexico. The laws that made slavery legal in the United States were not honored by Spain. Therefore, they were not honored by any of the Spanish territories such as Florida and Mexico, which comprised the nation's Southern borders. The Africans who escaped north to Canada became citizens and were protected by Canadian law from being returned to the United States and slavery. For fear of creating an international incident, very few white Americans crossed the Canadian border in pursuit of runaway slaves. Although Spain did not honor this country's laws regarding slavery, it did not prohibit white American slave hunters from capturing runaway slaves in Spanish territory and allowed the white slave hunters to return the slaves to the United States.

To avoid being captured by white slave hunters, slaves who had crossed into Spanish territory from Florida, turned to the Seminole Indian tribes for protection. The Seminoles were a Native American tribe whose habitat was the Everglades and swamps of what is now Florida. They were very sympathetic to the plight of the slaves because they shared a common enemy. That enemy was, of course, the white man. The shelter and safety provided to runaway slaves qualifies the Seminole tribesmen as freedom fighters.

Runaway slaves became members of Seminoles tribes, which resulted in a large number of Seminole and African interracial marriages. Eventually, the close relationship between red and black men and women would result in a mixed breed of Native American and African-American offsprings. The increasing number of runaway slaves increased the population of the Seminole tribe to such an extent that the Seminole Indians became known as the "Black Indian" tribes.

Not only were the slaves who escaped to Florida taken in by the Native Americans, but runaway slaves who crossed the Mississippi River and escaped to freedom in the West were aided by Native American tribes. The Native Americans and Africans shared the common experiences of having been abused by white Americans. This made the Native Americans a natural ally to many runaway slaves.

Unlike the covert actions of the white freedom fighters who conducted the Underground Railroad, the Seminoles did more than just provide food and shelter for the runaway slaves. The Seminoles combined with the runaway slaves to physically oppose the white slave hunters. The combination of Seminole tribesmen and free Africans formed an army that was able to combat the white slave hunters for years.

The Underground Railroad functioned under a non-violent doctrine. Because it was a non-violent system, historians have documented the adventures of the Underground Railroad and the efforts of the black members of this group

91

who worked to lead runaway slaves to freedom. The more violent struggles by slaves to gain their freedom received very little documentation and none of the glamorous recognition that historians gave to the non-violent Underground Railroad.

Because slaves were so valuable in America during this time, the army was directed to cross the border into the Spanish territory of Florida, capture and return them. History records that the government did not feel the army would meet with a great deal of resistance in its quest to Florida to return the slaves beause black men had never united to resist the authority of the white man. However, the military had vastly underestimated the strength of the runaway slaves combined with the Seminole warriors.

The Seminole tribesmen, who were accustomed to the terrain, mainly swamps and everglades, were able to mount a formidable resistance to the army. Historical records indicate that over 1,500 white soldiers lost their lives in the Seminole Indian wars before the army finally was able to return a significant number of runaway slaves.

The Civil War marked the end of slavery in America, and it also marked the end of the strong bond that had formed between the Native Americans and African Americans prior to the Civil War. After the slaves were freed from the plantations in the South, they found themselves suddenly without food and shelter or any other means of providing sustenance. The Civil War was very hard on this country's social and economic structure. It was exceptionally devastating to the social and economic framework of the former Confederate States of America. After the Civil War, there were very few jobs available in the South for white people, and there were hardly any jobs at all available for former slaves.

Free African men fought gallantly in the Union army during the Civil War. Prior to the Civil War, runaway slaves exhibited their proficiency in guerilla warfare when they joined the Seminole tribesmen to fight against the army in the Seminole Indian War. With this in mind, the government enlisted hundreds of former slaves and sent them west to fight in the Indian Wars. This provided jobs for the former slaves and additional troops for the army in its battle against the Native Americans. The wounds that led to the undoing of this bond between the red and black man would never be healed. Today, the once-close relationship between the Native Americans and African Americans still has not been restored. What destroyed the bond between the Native Americans and African Americans?

One hundred and fifty thousand African Americans served in the Union army during the Civil War. My grade school history lessons never included any mention of the African-American soldier's role in the Civil War, nor did they contain any information on black Americans ever serving in other wars. Remember, I started school in 1954. Then, black students were taught a strict white curriculum. Fortunately, I was able to learn from my ancestors the facts pertaining to the history of the African-American soldiers. I also had several members of my family who were career soldiers and had first-hand knowledge of the military. My relatives took the time to research the history of their chosen profession, which made it possible for them to pass this information along to me.

The former slaves were perfectly suited for the military lifestyle. As slaves, they were used to the long hours and stern discipline required to be a good soldier. What made the army a totally different experience for African Americans was the fact that they were now being paid for something they used to do for free. With freedom, the black man regained his pride and dignity. The renewed pride and dignity of African Americans played a major role in their becoming exceptional soldiers and superior Indian fighters.

Chapter Eight

In the years prior to the Civil War, Native Americans fought and died to protect the freedom of African Americans. What did we do to repay this debt? The answer to this question is absolutely nothing. After the Civil War, it is my opinion that the slaves should have joined the Native Americans in their fight against the white man or remained neutral. This may not have helped the red man win the war, but it may have avoided the alienation that still exists between Native Americans and black Americans.

I imagine Native Americans felt betrayed when the slaves, whom they had fought to protect, turned against them and fought on the side of the army. Although the Native Americans may have respected the "buffalo soldier" as a warrior, the red man could no longer trust or respect the black American as a friend. Trust is the most important part of any relationship between two humans.

What did the African Americans gain for betraying the Native Americans? The same reward Judas got for his betrayal of Jesus—a few pieces of silver. I can only offer this excuse for the conduct of my ancestors. They needed the army pay to support their families and buy the land that would provide for their future. Serving in the army was the only way the majority of the black Americans survived in the

West after the Civil War.

Although the black soldiers were paid for their service in the army, they received no additional rewards or benefits. The buffalo soldiers helped the army defeat the Indians in America, but the black man did not receive any added respect or additional rights from the white man.

The Native Americans treated us as their equals, and white Americans made us their slaves. It should have been an easy choice for the former slaves when it came to deciding on which side to fight in the Indian Wars. It would also appear to me that the black man in South Africa should have just as easy a choice in deciding between fighting for equality or being a member of the white South African army that defends apartheid.

The practice of apartheid would not exist in South Africa if it were not for the support of some black Africans. American apartheid could not survive without the blessing of some members of minority races who tolerate apartheid.

The buffalo soldiers were responsible for striking the deathblow that killed the kindred spirit that existed between the black man and the red man. As African Americans, we owe a great debt to the Native Americans, and it is incumbent upon us to do whatever it takes to heal the wounds that separate the black man and red man.

In order to win the war for racial equality, African Americans and Native Americans must rekindle the kindred spirit that existed between the two of them prior to the Civil War. This would enable the black man and red man to once again fight against their common enemy. That common enemy is racial discrimination and apartheid.

The Civil War was over. Slavery was no longer the law of the land, and the black man was free. If you would check an American dictionary from the late 1800's and the early 1900's, under the definition of a "free American," the definition of a free black man, a free red and a free white man would have totally different meanings in America. African Americans were free, but by no means were they equal to white Americans.

The black man was free, but the question was, "Free to do what or free to go where?" There were over 400,000 free black Americans or "non-slaves" living in the Northern states and Western territories about a century before the Civil War. Even more astonishing is the fact that about 100,000 "non-slaves" managed to survive in the deep South and enjoy a "quasi-free" lifestyle.

African Americans who were the offsprings of a white parent, former slaves who managed to save enough money to purchase their own freedom and black Americans who earned their freedom by serving in the military made up the majority of the "non-slave" population in America. This information is another one of the many known facts about the history of African Americans that was not taught to young black students when I was growing up.

Prior to the Emancipation Proclamation, white historians labeled the free black Americans as "non-slaves" or "quasi-free Negroes." The white man forced the Native Americans to live on reservations, and, although the "non-slaves" were not forced to live on reservations, the African Americans did form all-black communities out of the need for a support system. Because the free black Americans received little, if any, support from white America, the "quasi-free Negroes" set up a network of small farms and businesses in order to provide for their black families.

The "non-slaves" of the North and West did have a head start on the slaves of the South when it came to freedom; however, the "non-slaves" in America were not entirely free and were never considered equal to the white man. In fact, the "quasi-free Negroes" had to carry a document on them at all times verifying that they were legally free. They had to produce these papers any time they were challenged by a white man. If a "non-slave" who was born a free man did not have credentials to confirm his freedom, he could be arrested and condemned to a life of slavery.

African Americans no longer had to endure the physical and mental abuse of the white slave masters or be restricted to living within the boundaries of a plantation. You would think that, as soon as the slaves were freed, they would have gone as far away from the South as possible. However, after more than 200 years of slavery and life on a plantation, most black Americans were not able to handle the sudden changes associated with freedom. For former African slaves, being free was not easy.

In a perfect world, the government would have arranged for the recently-freed slaves to be debriefed. The government should have made it a requirement for all former slaves to attend an in-depth orientation on how to be a free citizen. What the government intended, as compensation for all the years the black man suffered as a slave, was to give each freed slave 40 acres and a mule to start a new life in the unsettled Western territory. The government never kept its promise of 40 acres and a mule. There were not enough mules and enough land to give every slave 40 acres and a mule. Just think of the economic impact today if each African American would have received the 40 acres from the government.

How did the government expect the slaves, who had been denied the right to an education, to survive? Most former slaves could not read or write. The lack of a formal education became an even greater handicap for the former slaves because of their limited command of the English language. Many former slaves' inability to fluently communicate with white Americans limited their career opportunities to low-skilled jobs or manual labor.

Rather than leave the South after the Civil War, many slaves remained on the plantations and became migrant workers. Picking cotton, cutting sugar cane and tobacco required very little skill and no education. These were the only jobs available for the former slaves in the South. Being a black migrant worker in the South after the Civil War was only a step above slavery. Just like slaves, the black migrant workers worked long hours for low wages. Black people were no longer the property of the white plantation owner, but they still had control over their capability of surviving in the South.

The first actual black Civil Rights Movement began in the United States after the Civil War. This Civil Rights Movement was part of what was known as "Reconstruction." It was called that because the South actually had to be reconstructed after the Civil War. The Union army left the South, for lack of a better word, in one big "mess." As in the classic movie, "Gone With The Wind," gone were most of the vast acres of plantations along with their huge mansions. The Confederacy had been defeated, and the "old-fashioned" lifestyle of white Americans was shattered.

As a result of the confusion in the South during Reconstruction, African Americans were able to take advantage of this situation and gain a great deal of political power. The former slave population, with the aid of so-called white "carpetbaggers" from the North, made the Republican Party the dominant political power in the reconstructed South. African Americans became prominent figures in local and state government. These black politicians were able to promote legislation that helped to improve the living conditions for African Americans. The most beneficial improvements were made in the areas of education and the right to vote.

After hundreds of years of being denied an education, a school system for former slaves was now available in

AMERICAN APARTHEID

the South. For the first time in most areas, black Americans were learning how to read, write and effectively use the English language. These extremely vital achievements in education would be the motivating factor behind the modern Civil Rights Movement. Remember, knowledge is power, and education is the key to knowledge.

The Republican Party continued to encourage African Americans to take an active role in the election of public officials, and this would lead to an increasing number of black representatives in government. The fact that the Republican Party supported the early Civil Rights Movement is the reason it became the political party of choice for most African Americans from the 1860's through the early 1930's. It was during Reconstruction that the first African American, Blanche K. Bruce of Mississippi, was elected to the United States Senate. The fact that in 1874 Senator Bruce became the first black person to serve in the Senate was a significant accomplishment for blacks. However, it was just as big of a setback for African Americans when P.B.S. Pinchback, a black man, was elected from Louisiana in 1874 to fill a seat in the Senate, and the white senators in Washington voted not to allow this black man to fill the seat.

The government's action that denied Mr. Pinchback his right to serve in the Senate came at the end of Reconstruction. Not only was the South reconstructed, the white Southern Democratic political machine was back in power and stronger than ever. During Reconstruction, black Americans in the South had experienced the sweet taste of that same political power. They were hungry for more and were determined not to lose the control they had gained. In order for the white apartheid system to regain its dominance over blacks in the South, it organized white radical groups that used violence and fear as a method to force black Southerners to give up their political power.

White militant organizations used violent intimidation tactics such as arson, murder and vandalism to convince blacks not to vote in local elections or to leave town. With the help of groups such as the "White Brotherhood," the "White Camelia," the "Pale Faces" and the notorious "Knights of the Ku Klux Klan," the white political regime was able to reenact the "Black Code." The so-called "Black Code" was a set of laws that made it almost impossible for Southern African Americans to qualify to vote. This code had not been invoked in the South since before the Civil War. It was very difficult for Southern African Americans to combat these white militant groups because they were supported by local law enforcement. In some cases, even the local white sheriff was a member of the Klan.

The local white governments passed a set of voter registration rules and regulations that only applied to black voters. The problem African Americans encountered when they attempted to comply with the requirements to vote, which were established by this white apartheid system, was that the rules always managed to change just enough so no matter what a black man did he could not meet the qualifications to register to vote.

Black Americans took this obvious case of racial discrimination to the U.S. Supreme Court, as it was clearly a violation of the 15th amendment to the Constitution. The court basically ruled that the government did not have the right to interfere in local politics. In 1875, the court ruled that the 15th amendment only guaranteed that a state could not discriminate against anyone based on race, color or previous condition of servitude; however, the 15th amendment did not guarantee anyone the right to vote. The lack of support from the Supreme Court and the broader government, in general, ended any hope of the African American's return to Southern political power.

Just as apartheid on the African continent is concentrated in South Africa, the focus of racial discrimination for African Americans has always been in the South. However, black Americans who live in other geographical areas of America face the same racial obstacles as Southern African Americans. Blacks who lived in the deep South migrated to the Northern and Western regions of the United States in hopes of finding better living conditions and equal opportunity. What they found was that the only difference in these other regions of the country was that racial discrimination against black Americans was not as blatant or obvious as it was in the South.

Chapter Nine

The Civil Rights Movement for African Americans all but came to a standstill in America between the end of Reconstruction and the end of World War II. The civil rights organizations made numerous attempts at making changes in the white apartheid system, but their efforts were met with resistance from the strong white conservative government that was in power in America during this time period.

Although African Americans may not have made any major breakthroughs in gaining equal rights for approximately 50 years after Reconstruction, black Americans did make some noticeable strides in the area of education. The increase in educational opportunities for black Americans became the driving force behind the resurgence of the modern Civil Rights Movement. As young black men and women became better educated, they also became dissatisfied with their status as second-class citizens.

The study of African-American history is one of the most interesting subjects one could ever study. It would be a shame if young Americans were denied the opportunity to learn about such famous black Americans as: George Washington Carver, Frederick Douglass, Benjamin Banneker, Mary McLeod Bethune, Booker T. Washington, Paul

Laurence Dunbar and W.E.B. Dubois. These African-American scholars and educators are directly linked to the modern-day Civil Rights Movement, and they are credited with the infusion of knowledge that helped create a major attitude adjustment in black men and women throughout America.

Due to the efforts of these and other eminent African American educators and scholars, blacks were now able to effectively interpret and evaluate the law. As a result of their education, African Americans began to examine the laws established by the white apartheid system. Not only did black scholars begin to examine these laws, they began to question the validity of any legislation that made it legal to deny an individual his or her rights based on race. It was the black educators and scholars in America who planted the seeds for the birth of such powerful civil rights organizations as the NAACP, the National Association for the Advancement of Colored People, and the National Urban League.

I thank the black American scholars and educators who had this subtle, yet powerful, influence on future civil rights workers in America. In my opinion, these great educators and scholars were the foreparents of the concept of non-violence and peaceful negotiations, which was the doctrine of the modern Civil Rights Movement.

The history of the following black institutions of higher learning will give you a better perspective of the accomplishments of our great African-American educators and scholars: Howard University, Hampton Institute, Meharry Medical Institute, Morehouse College, Tuskegee Institute, Bethune-Cookman College and Fisk University.

There were some black Americans whose impatience with the white apartheid system caused them to take a more aggressive approach to change the system—the white apartheid system. A pugnacious young African American named Jack Johnson challenged the white sports promoters who controlled boxing , and he became the first black man to fight a white man for the world's heavyweight boxing championship. Since the days of John L. Sullivan, the world's heavyweight champion was glorified as the most glamorous athlete in sports, and he was exalted as being physically superior to any man in the world.

When you mention great heavyweight boxing champions, two names usually come to mind: Joe Louis and Muhammad Ali. Very seldom do you hear the name Jack Johnson, who may have been the greatest heavyweight boxer of all time. When white sportswriters in America talk about this great boxer, they always seem to focus on the negative highlights of Johnson's boxing career and fail to emphasize the fact that he dominated the boxing like no other man had done before and no other man has done since.

Johnson was an imposing physical presence who used his skills as a boxer to intimidate the world. He was an arrogant black man who openly defied the white apartheid system. He frequently disregarded the law by speeding around the country in his big expensive car, and he incurred the wrath of the white male population by dating white women. What made Johnson's brash exploits even more of a thorn in the side of white America was that as the heavyweight champion, everything he did made world-wide newspaper headlines. Just imagine how it made most white men feel in the 1900's to see a picture of a black man, Jack Johnson, in their morning papers holding a white woman in his arms.

In the early 1900's, when Johnson easily defeated America's white heavyweight champion, he immediately became a source of embarrassment for the white apartheid supporters and a positive role model and inspiration for all black people in America. The fact that an African-American male held the World Heavyweight Boxing Championship was incredible. It was the closest thing to a black man being elected President. Black Americans could now look at the success of Jack Johnson and feel they could accomplish anything the white man had accomplished.

In the late 1960's, African Americans frequently used the phrase "Black is Beautiful" as an expression of racial pride. The originator of the phrase "Black is Beautiful" was an African American named Marcus Garvey. Before the Nation of Islam, also known as "Black Muslims," began to preach to African Americans about racial pride and separation from the white man in America, Marcus Garvey had already started delivering the message to black people in most of the major East Coast cities.

Garvey exhorted African Americans to become independent. He urged black people to separate themselves from the white apartheid system that refused to treat them as equals and establish their own country where they could be truly free. In my opinion, Marcus Garvey was the father of the black militant movement. He encouraged African Americans to be proud of who they were and of their racial heritage.

In 1919, over 500,000 African Americans had joined Garvey's movement to establish independence. His plan was for all black Americans to move back to Africa and develop a new country. Garvey spent millions of dollars building a fleet of ocean liners to take blacks back to Africa. Unlike the efforts of some of the other black leaders of this time period, his plan was financially supported, in part, by the white apartheid system that encouraged the movement of black Americans back to Africa. However, Garvey was unable to convince enough of the black American population to buy passage on his ocean liners, and, as a result, his efforts failed.

In the 1930s, the Nation of Islam, under the leadership of the Honorable Elijah Muhammad, would rekindle the spirit of the movement originated by Marcus Garvey, which encouraged black Americans not to depend on the white man for survival and to completely separate themselves from white America. The Nation of Islam is responsible for establishing a number of independently-owned small businesses in the black community that are still in operation today. The Nation of Islam, using a strong religious doctrine and a sound economic philosophy, was able to establish a firm foundation for the Black Muslim organization in African-American communities.

My personal choice for the most impressive African-American male role model of the 1930's and 1940's was Paul Leroy Bustill Robeson. He was a black visionary, a "Renaissance Man," whose only problem was that he was born far ahead of his time. I wish there was some popular figure in American history that Paul Robeson could be compared to in order to give some indication as to why he was so awe-inspiring. To say he was a combination of Jim Brown, John Wayne and Pavarotti, may be a hint of how impressed I am by the late Paul Robeson, but it still does not give justice to this great American.

What made Paul Robeson so special was the fact that he refused to accept the stereotypical role that the white apartheid system had always reserved for talented black artists. He was a proud black man who demanded to be treated as an equal to any other man regardless of the color of his skin, and he refused to be denied his rights as a citizen. Like Jack Johnson, Paul Robeson could intimidate people with his physical stature, but his intellect and oratory skills made a greater impression than his physical attributes.

During his college days, Robeson lettered in baseball, basketball and track. He was an All-American football player and a Phi Beta Kappa, who graduated with honors from Rutgers University. He earned a law degree from Columbia University, and, in 1923, he became a member of the New York State Bar Association. He was an accomplished actor who starred on the live stage and in motion pictures and spoke over 20 languages. He was a world-famous baritone who performed in operas throughout America and Europe, and his most famous role was that of Othello. It was said of him that there was nothing in this world a man could do that he could not do better.

Although Robeson won numerous awards for his efforts in the area of civil rights, he was not a leader in the battle for racial equality. He acted as an individual who was aggressive and very outspoken in his maligning of the white apartheid system that attempted to damper his spirit and detour his rise in America. Before the likes of Paul Robeson, black America had not witnessed such a forthright approach to equality by an African American.

Just as Jack Johnson had to be defeated because he was a threat to white supremacy in America, so did the white supporters of apartheid have to destroy Paul Robeson. Ironically, the white supremacy groups used the same method to defeat both men. They took away the things they loved most. They would not allow Johnson to defend his title, and they would not allow Robeson to be an actor.

Not being able to find work as an actor in America, Robeson found a welcome audience for his skills in Europe. Although he was not a Communist, Robeson settled for a time in Russia. This move gave white America all the ammunition it needed to brand him a Communist and to discredit him not only among white Americans but African Americans as well. It has only been since his death in 1976 that black Americans realized white America labeled Paul Robeson a Communist so he would not become a positive role model. More recently, black Americans have also come to realize that Robeson was an exceptional human being.

The big stumbling block that kept the Civil Rights

Movement from gaining the momentum it needed to be more successful during the period between 1900 through 1945 was the lack of support from President Theodore Roosevelt. Civil rights groups worked hard to get federal equal rights legislation introduced in the House of Representatives and the Senate, only to have the President turn a deaf ear to the request from civil rights leaders for his support in getting this legislation passed.

Take a look at the record of the presidents who held office between 1900 and 1948. Just think about the significant changes in racial equality that took place during this same time period and name the president who was responsible for that change. If you are having a difficult time trying to think of some of these monumental changes that affected race relations in America, do not despair because they were very few and far between.

In 1900, President William McKinley gave African Americans a reason to rejoice and a reason to have high expectations for their future when he appointed a record number of blacks to federal positions. After McKinley's death in 1901, Theodore Roosevelt became president, and he made it clear that he would not be replacing any African Americans who were appointed to federal positions by President McKinley. Mr. Roosevelt was credited with saying, "The color of a man's skin was no reason for him to lose his job." President Roosevelt's actions caused some black Americans to call him the best president since Abraham Lincoln. Black Americans who compared President Roosevelt and President Lincoln are like chickens trying to choose what feels better, the skillet or the frying pan.

African Americans would soon find that, like President Lincoln, President Theodore Roosevelt had more concern for what was best for the country and very little consideration for the plight of black people. During President

Roosevelt's administration, African Americans suffered the worst setback since the days of slavery. They were being forced off their land in states throughout the South and Midwest. White Americans in the Northern states, who had been supportive of African Americans during the abolition of slavery, were now practicing the simple tactics of racial hatred that was the trademark of white Southerners.

After President Roosevelt, black Americans did not trust President Taft, and they got only lip service from President Woodrow Wilson. The white apartheid system in America, which featured total white supremacy, had started a reign of terror. Black Americans were being publicly lynched, burned and murdered by white militants while the President stood by and did nothing to stop this injustice. Over 20 bills proposing legislation against racial discrimination and racial violence were introduced in Congress while President Wilson was in office. None of them passed.

Something African Americans can attribute to President Wilson was an Executive Order that segregated federal employees dining and rest room facilities. When black American leaders met with the President to complain about his segregationist actions, they were quickly dismissed because he felt their questioning of an Executive Order was a personal insult. This president will also be remembered for ordering the Marine Corps to invade Haiti because the Haitian government was out of control. The invasion of this sovereign country resulted in the death of hundreds of Haitians. After reading this fact, you may ask why President Wilson would order the invasion of Haiti? The reason was to protect democracy. The government has gone into countries such as Haiti and Cuba to protect democracy. We went into Korea and Viet Nam to stop the spread of Communism. I wonder why the government didn't go into South Africa to stop the spread of apartheid.

Between 1920 and 1932, America elected several presidents, none of whom did anything to slow the roll of the terrorist's white apartheid juggernaut or improve the living conditions of African Americans. Black Americans either enlisted or were drafted into the armed services to fight in World War I. As all the black soldiers before World War I, the black soldiers who fought and died in World War I faced segregation and were denied equal rights. The entire country went through a long Depression, and, maybe for the first time in America, some white people felt the hopelessness and despair that black people had been experiencing for over two 200 years.

World War I was over, and America was recovering from the great Depression. In 1932, President Franklin D. Roosevelt was elected. FDR was president for four consecutive terms, serving 12 years in office, longer than any other president. Some historians feel Franklin D. Roosevelt was the greatest president. There are tons of documents that chronicle the brilliant achievements of President Roosevelt during his years in office. What I found to be more interesting were things that Mr. Roosevelt did not accomplish while he was in office.

If you talk to black Americans who lived through the Roosevelt era, they may agree that FDR was a great president. In my opinion, he was a better politician than a president. FDR realized that African Americans were now a political force in America, and, therefore, he made a number of federal appointments to appease black Americans. FDR, a clever politician, formed a "Negro Cabinet," African Americans from around the country, to advise him on matters regarding their interests.

President Roosevelt's "Negro Cabinet" took black America back to the days of slavery when the white plantation owners would have the so-called "house niggers" spy on the field slaves. The information obtained from his Negro Cabinet or the "White House niggers" helped FDR to convince African Americans to switch from the Republican Party, their traditional choice, to the Democratic Party. The trouble with black people during this period was that they were satisfied with whatever little tidbit of hope for equality the occupant of the White House threw their way.

What most black Americans who lived during FDR's administration probably never knew was that more African Americans were lynched while he was president than during the term of any other president in history after the Civil War. Mr. Roosevelt, for fear of upsetting white Southern politicians, refused to support an anti-lynching bill that was submitted to Congress by a group of black congressmen. The only legitimate support for racial equality generated from the White House during FDR's administration came from Mrs. Eleanor Roosevelt, the First Lady. She openly supported equal rights for blacks. The account of Mrs. Roosevelt's flight with the Tuskegee airmen, a group of black army pilots, is one example.

Chapter Ten

World War II marked the beginning of a positive shift in momentum for the Civil Rights Movement. Black Americans began to unite in a common effort to change the racist attitudes of the white apartheid system. During World War II, General Dwight David Eisenhower, commander of the allied troops in Europe, ordered the desegregation of all European-based American armed forces. For the first time, black and white soldiers not only fought together on the battlefields, they slept in the same barracks, used the same rest rooms and ate in the same dining halls.

General Eisenhower unselfishly risked his military career and his political future when he went across the grain of the white apartheid system and ordered the desegregation of the troops under his command. In my opinion, the desegregation of the America's military ranks as one of the most outstanding event in African-American history since the Emancipation Proclamation. This bold move made General Eisenhower one of my great American heroes. It is personally disheartening that the general, who went on to become president, does not receive the credit he deserves for this accomplishment and contribution in the area of racial equality in America.

The United States felt the full impact of the deseg-regation of the military after World War II was over, and over a million black soldiers returned to America. The black soldiers who left America to fight in Europe were just naive young boys, but they returned to America as seasoned war veterans. These seasoned black war veterans, who had tasted the respect and freedom of being equal to the white man in the military, were not about to tolerate the bigotry of white apartheid America.

Along with the black war veterans, there emerged some African-American sports figures who were breaking racial barriers. Jackie Robinson and Joe Louis helped prove to America that, if given the opportunity, a black man could compete in professional sports. Jackie Robinson, the first African American to play in the major leagues, went on to become Rookie of the Year and the National League's Most Valuable Player. Joe Louis became an American hero when he knocked out Max Schmelling, the heavyweight cham-pion and the pride of Nazi Germany.

The next blockbuster in America's Civil Rights Movement came in 1954 when the United States Supreme Court ruled that segregated schools were unconstitutional. School desegregation brought the battle for racial equality to the front lines. Black leaders such as Charles Houston and Thurgood Marshall, a future Supreme Court justice, were responsible for presenting to the court the issue of segre-gated schools being unequal. School systems throughout America were now being forced to integrate their schools or lose federal funding. The desegregation of schools in the South started a full-scale war between the white supremacy supporters and the civil rights organizations. Guess who was president when the Supreme Court ruled segregated schools were unconstitutional? Yes, the desegregation of schools was another feather in the cap of my hero, President Dwight

David Eisenhower.

Despite heavy resistance from the white supporters of apartheid, many schools across the country were integrated. African-American students, often protected by federal marshals or National Guardsmen, were bused into white neighborhoods to attend school. In predominantly black neighborhoods, schools received additional state and federal funding to improve the facilities as well as purchase better books and equipment. Unfortunately, African Americans still feel pain and have physical and mental scars from the battle for school desegregation. Black Americans, however, can find comfort in the fact that their suffering was not in vain and that school desegregation was a major victory in the war for racial equality in America.

Ralph Branca is the answer to the popular trivia question: Who was the pitcher for the Brooklyn Dodgers in 1951 when Bobby Thompson hit the home run for the New York Giants to win the National League pennant? A trivia question that I would love to know the answer to is: Who was the white man that tried to take Rosa Parks's seat on the bus? Whoever he is, his name should be recorded in African-American history for his contribution to the Civil Rights Movement in America. If the white man who wanted Rosa Parks to give him her seat on the bus had any idea of what would be the result of his demand, I think he would have stood on a bus from Montgomery, Alabama to Washington D.C.

When the black citizens decided to boycott the mass transit system and not ride the buses in Montgomery until the city ended the practice of racial discrimination, they found that money was a route to end an evil. The organized boycott almost bankrupted the bus company and forced the white city officials to concede to the demands of the city's black citizens. The Montgomery boycott became a model for civil rights workers. It showed how an organized peaceful demonstration by black citizens supported by white Americans could accomplish a realistic goal.

Most Americans saw the 1991 video tape of Rodney King being inhumanly battered by police officers in Los Angeles. Police brutality was the hot topic of conversation in households throughout America, including the White House. The police officers who beat Rodney King violated his civil rights, and most Americans were appalled at this blatant act of cruelty.

The police stopped Rodney King after a high speed chase. According to police reports, Mr. King was traveling at speeds close to 100 miles per hour, which made him a danger to himself and others. He was driving under the influence of drugs and/or alcohol, and he initially refused to stop his vehicle when directed to do so by a police officer. If you believe the police reports, Rodney King was obviously breaking the law, but he still did not deserve the beating he received from the police.

According to published reports, King is an ex-convict with a record of arrests for possession of illegal drugs. Indeed, he was not a model citizen, yet all America felt sorry for him. I remember another King, Martin Luther King, civil rights leader and Nobel Prize winner, whose assassination in Memphis, Tennessee, in my opinion, did not receive as much attention as the Rodney King beating in Los Angeles.

If you were upset by the Rodney King beating, check out some live news coverage from the peaceful civil rights demonstrations in the South during the late 1950's, the 1960's or the early 1970's. Southern white police officers used clubs to beat viciously black civil rights demonstrators. The bloody faces of these young black men and women, as police kicked, beat them and had police dogs attack them, became an all-too-familiar sight on the evening news reports.

115

Although America witnessed constant visual accounts of unmerciful acts of brutality by white police on black civil rights workers, there was very little done to stop these inhuman police tactics. The "good ole boy" network of Southern politicians created a roadblock of red tape to keep the government from sending federal troops to protect the civil rights workers in the South. It was President John F. Kennedy, black America's "Great White Hope" for racial equality, who used his power as Commander-in-Chief to order troops to protect the civil rights workers.

Because of his support for the Civil Rights Movement, some historians like to compare President Kennedy to President Lincoln, who used slavery as a pawn in the chess game to keep the secessionists from leaving the Union. He was not concerned with the equal rights of African Americans but for the unity of this country.

In my opinion, it is an insult to the memory of President Kennedy to even associate his accomplishments as president to those of Lincoln. Mr. Kennedy won the support of the black voters by promising to work toward ending racial discrimination. Once elected, the President used the power of his office to keep his promise to his African-American voters by supporting the civil rights legislation in Congress.

In the 1960's, white America could feel the walls of apartheid about to crumble and fall. What could the white supporters of apartheid do to save their precious system of white supremacy in America? It is my most ardent opinion that President Kennedy, Dr. King, Malcolm X and Robert Kennedy were all assassinated to slow the momentum of the Civil Rights Movement. Historians labeled these killings assassinations, but, in my opinion, they were merely the acts of gutless cowards who shot down defenseless victims and should not be glorified with the word assassinate. Senseless

116

murders by any other name are just as tragic.

Like many other Americans, I strongly feel there was a conspiracy to murder all the aforementioned men, and the list of possible suspects who could have organized this conspiracy include, but are not limited to: the Ku Klux Klan, the Federal Bureau of Investigation and the American Nazi Party. After reading this list of suspects, I know you are probably asking the question, what does the FBI have in common with the KKK and the Nazi party?

In my opinion, there may have been some other government agencies involved in this conspiracy, but I included the FBI because of the racist reputation of J. Edgar Hoover and his much-publicized dislike of the Kennedy family. During the height of the Civil Rights Movement in the 1960's, Mr. Hoover was the Director of the Federal Bureau of Investigation and one of the most powerful men in Washington. Mr. Hoover had an on-going feud with the Kennedy brothers, and he felt both Dr. King and Malcolm X were Communists.

Reportedly, Mr. Hoover ordered the FBI to conduct investigations into the private and personal lives of these murder victims in an effort to dig up some dirt that might discredit them in the eyes of America. It would not come as a surprise to me if someday an official government report was released that implicated the FBI, under the direction of Mr. Hoover, in the assassination of the Kennedys, Dr. King and Malcolm X.

The battle for equal rights in America is, indeed, a war, and the army of civil rights workers lost its most influential leaders in the 1960's when John and Robert Kennedy, Malcolm X and Dr. King were killed. Although each of these slain civil rights leaders used a different strategy in their approach to end racial discrimination, they were all very effective in accomplishing this goal.

I feel fortunate enough to have lived during the time of these great Americans; I will miss them.

Dr. King used the peaceful demonstration as his weapon of choice in the fight to gain equality for African Americans. Malcolm X used a more aggressive approach in his battle plan to end racial discrimination. He felt black Americans had been patient long enough and should no longer have to wait for the white man to decide when, where, and how to accept them as equals in America. Malcolm X felt the black man must demand equality and defend his right to be equal by any means necessary. President Kennedy and Attorney General Kennedy fought their battles for civil rights in political arenas. In my opinion, the reason these men were murdered was to keep them from ever uniting as one force in the battle to end racial discrimination.

In his famous "I Have a Dream" speech, Dr. King gave a strong indication that he was tired of the slow progress of the peaceful demonstration, and it may have been time to try another method to gain equality. This speech came shortly after he had agreed to a meeting with Malcolm X to discuss the possibility of working together. The Kennedys had already gone on record as supporting the Civil Rights Movement and Dr. King. If the civil right workers who followed Dr. King's direction could be united with the members of the Nation of Islam who were loyal to Malcolm X, they would have formed an unstoppable army of civil rights workers. The white apartheid system would have been defeated, and overt racial discrimination would no longer have exist in America.

The war to end racial discrimination appears to be a never-ending battle. Although there has been some progress over the years, the Civil Rights Movement has not recovered from the loss of its great leader. The battle for racial equality in America has gone from the full-scale war of the late 1950's to small skirmishes being fought mainly by the NAACP in the 1990's. Native Americans, Hispanic Americans, African Americans and other minority races all continue to fight for equality as individuals and not as a united group to defeat a common foe.

It is impossible to replace such leaders as Dr. Martin King, Malcolm X, and the Kennedys. However, we must protect their memory and not let their deaths be in vain. We are now the soldiers in the war to end racial discrimination and apartheid. We must continue to battle with the same zest and zeal as those aforementioned slain generals. We must rekindle their spirit, and all Americans, regardless of the color of their skin, must join together, work toward a better America and help make the dreams of these slain civil rights leaders come true.

Chapter Eleven

"...With liberty and justice for all."

If you do not recognize this quote, it is from the Pledge of Allegiance to the flag. When I was in grammar school, every morning before starting class, we had to repeat the Pledge of Allegiance. I used this quote to make a point about the phrase "...justice for all." Are African Americans part of the population in this country that makes up the "all" as in "justice for all"? The late African-American comedian Redd Foxx used to tell a joke about black people going to court: "If a black man goes to court looking for justice in this country, the only people he will find standing trial is just—us."

When I first heard this joke, I laughed because I thought it was very funny. As I began to think about the justice system in America, I realized it was hardly a laughing matter. Although Redd Foxx may have said it in jest, it is far too real a fact of life that the majority of the people who end up in court in this country are members of a minority race. The justice system is a perfect example that the racist influence of apartheid is still alive and well.

This is another of my true-life experiences. On June 10, 1994, I went to traffic court to contest a speeding ticket. The district court was located in a small rural community in Maryland's Baltimore County. As I waited for my case to be called, I started to think about the Redd Foxx joke. I began to count the number of African Americans in the courtroom. Twenty-three of the 60 people in the courtroom were black, three were Asian Americans, and the remaining number were white.

Was it just a strange coincidence that, in a predominantly white neighborhood, 38 percent of the citizens in the courtroom were African Americans? I was about to dismiss the issue as just that, a strange coincidence, before the judge called the black state trooper who had given me a ticket to begin hearing his cases for the day.

The judge, who was white, started to call the names of the people to whom this trooper had given traffic tickets. Of the first 15 names called, ten of the people who came forward were black, the other five failed to appear for court that day. The reality of this situation suddenly hit home. I realized that this was no coincidence. I was now a witness, and soon to be a victim of the impact of American apartheid on the justice system. After the trooper read from the notes he had made on the back of each ticket, the judge found all 10 people guilty. The next five people called by the judge were also black, and all were found guilty.

The judge finally called the name of a white man who had been issued a traffic citation by the black trooper. The white man's plea was not guilty and the black trooper, who had referred to his notes to get 15 straight guilty verdicts, looked at the judge and said he had no notes for this case. Operating the same radar unit he used to issue all his other citations, the trooper stated that he wrote this white man a citation for exceeding the posted speed limit. According to the trooper, the man's vehicle was traveling at a speed of 76 mph in a 55 mph zone. After that brief statement, the black trooper told the judge he had no other information regarding this particular traffic stop.

It was as obvious as the nose on my face that the white man had made some prior arrangement with the court that was about to allow him to beat the system. Somehow, the white man had arranged for the black trooper conveniently to forget his notes, which allowed the judge to find him not guilty. As the white man was leaving the courtroom, the judge looked up from his bench and told him, "Have a nice day." It was as if the judge were saying, "See, I told you I would take care of everything."

As I left the court after being found guilty, I was very angry and frustrated. I was not the least bit upset over the fact that I was found guilty of a minor traffic offense. However, I was furious over the fact that I had just been a victim of an obvious case of racial injustice. Although my experience in the courtroom can in no way compare to the racial injustice endured by my ancestors, or to that of the black South Africans, I felt I had the right to be upset. The thought of black South African soldiers defending the white apartheid system and black slaves fighting to preserve the Confederacy came to mind as a reflection of the black trooper helping a white judge use his power to abuse African Americans.

Why would an African-American state trooper became a pawn in this racist system of justice? How could a white judge in a small traffic court commit such obvious acts of racial discrimination? I wanted to stand in court and scream that enough is enough. The reason I did not protest this act of racial injustice was because none of the other African Americans in court seemed to care. Sometimes, I think black people have become so accustomed to being discriminated against that we become like lambs heading to the slaughter, and we accept racism as if it is our destiny.

Prior to the Civil War, white plantation owners used a strong black male slave, commonly called "Roebuck," to supervise the other slaves. In the absence of the plantation owner, it was the "Roebuck's" duty to ensure that the white master's rules were obeyed by the other slaves. This black trooper, like many other black Americans today, still have the "Roebuck" mentality and feel it is their responsibility to make sure that African Americans do not break the white man's rules. Although I was totally disgusted, I just paid my fine and left the building. End of story.

The symbol for justice in America is the statue of a lady with a blindfold over her eyes holding a balanced scale. According to my high school civics, the scale and the blind-fold signify that the justice system in America is fair and impartial. There are tons of documented court cases that support the fact that the scales of justice for Native Americans and African Americans never have been balanced, and, even though she may be blind, the eyes of justice have always been able to tell the difference among red, brown, black and white.

Why do we have one system of justice in this country for white Americans and another system of justice for non-white Americans? Can non-whites ever get a "fair" trial in America? Has a non-white American ever really faced a jury of his or her peers? These are just a few questions to think about as you continue to read this chapter.

The same white apartheid mentality that would not share America with the Native Americans and made African Americans slaves also created a justice system that was designed to protect the rights of white Americans against any claims of injustice from non-white Americans. Are the white Americans who support apartheid so ignorant to the truth that they cannot recognize the problems with the American justice system? Is the justice system the last barrier left to keep white Americans and non-white Americans from becoming totally equal in this country?

A fair and impartial justice system would remove the

final barrier that keeps apartheid alive in this country. In my opinion, if the government would enforce the true concept of "justice for all," it would open up the possibility of racial equality in America. Is this a scary thought or what? *Even the most liberal sector of white America may not be ready for total racial equality.*

The Native Americans were the first to be victimized by the apartheid system of justice in America. I have already expressed my strong opinions about the injustice endured by the Native Americans. However, if you look at the so-called, and what is now famous, purchase of Manhattan from the Indians for what amounted to $24 dollars, this is another example of injustice. What court in the world would have upheld that contract as being a legal transaction? The Native Americans were the first to refer to America's justice system as the "white man's law," which was a very accurate description of the system then and is still an accurate description today.

Prior to the Civil War, some white slave owners were actually arrested in some Southern states for brutally murdering black slaves. Although black slaves were routinely whipped to death or lynched by white slave owners, it was the burning or chopping up of black slaves into pieces that even white Southerners could not tolerate. White slave owners were often found guilty of these brutal acts of murder. However, the righteous indignation of these white Southerners was easily tempered by the racial bias of the Southern justice system. The slave owners who were found guilty of murder were merely given a small fine by the local magistrate or sentenced to a few days in the local jail for killing a slave.

In most cases, both the fine and the jail sentence were usually suspended. The only real punishment suffered by the white slave owner for these inhuman acts against black

Americans was the embarrassment of being hauled into court for a crime committed against a slave. Just think, some people actually felt public ridicule was punishment enough for the murder of a black American in this country. Have things really changed that much over the past 200 years?

There was no way a white judge would severely punish a white man for any crime committed against a black person. Prior to the Civil War, a verbal slap on the wrist or a small fine were the strongest penalties imposed on any white man convicted of a crime against a black man. It may be hard to believe, but this is a fact and part of our American history. On the other hand, any crime committed by a red or black man against a white person resulted in a death sentence.

When confronted with these facts about our justice system, regardless of their race, most people will use the excuse, "That only happened in the old days, and it could never happen today." However, the problem with that excuse is it has been used for over 200 years, and the racial bias in America's justice system still exists. When is America going to wake up to the fact that we have a double standard in our justice system? When is black America going to wake up and realize that there will be no equality in the justice system in this country until we demand a change? African Americans thought the justice system in this country would change after the Emancipation Proclamation, but it did not. Black Americans were soon to find that, although the "white man's law" had made them free, it had in no way made them equal to the white man in America.

I sometimes feel the Constitution should have been written on toilet paper. Why toilet paper? The reason I say this is because the words used to make up the laws written in the Constitution have very little substance when it comes to how they apply to black people in this country. At least if it had been written on toilet paper, black Americans may have found a better use for the Constitution. We could use the toilet paper to wipe our butts rather than have the laws in the Constitution, which only apply to white people in America, shoved down our throats.

In order to have a fair and impartial justice system in America, we must start by enforcing the Constitution in the spirit of the Declaration of Independence. For most black people, the laws written in the Constitution, which are supposed to ensure and protect the rights of all Americans, have never been enforced equally for African Americans. The Declaration of Independence declares for all citizens, regardless of race, color, creed or national origin, the right to life, liberty and the pursuit of happiness. By the way, the Constitution guarantees the right to due process under the law in our justice system.

The Constitution should be enforced by the government by whatever means necessary. That being the case, black Americans, whose rights are guaranteed by the Constitution, would not continue to have their rights violated by the white man while the government watches from a ringside seat. The government failed to protect the Fourth Amendment rights of the peaceful demonstrator or civil rights workers who had fire hoses, attack dogs and night sticks used on them by local law enforcement officers in the South. The government's excuse for not investigating crimes involving racial violence was it never had any evidence. I could never understand how it could use that excuse when the crimes were being committed on nationwide television networks. Whatever happened to a picture speaking louder than a thousand words?

Chapter Twelve

Are we asking for too much when we say that a black man should expect to have his Constitutional rights protected in America? Are we asking for too much when we say a black man should be considered innocent until proven guilty in this country? Are freedom, justice, and equality really too much to ask for any American?

Is it actually possible for the white justice system in America to presume an African American to be innocent until proven guilty in a court of law? The white social structure in this country has stereotyped all black people as criminals; therefore, it is almost impossible for white America to see a black man as being innocent. Why is it that a large segment of the white population in America still believes that all black people lie, cheat, steal and carry a knife or gun? In a recent televised survey done on racism in this country, one of the white man's greatest fears in America is that his wife or daughter may be assaulted or raped by a black man.

Wake up white people! Black people are the ones who should be in fear. Did someone forget that we are the minority race in this country? We are the ones who are being denied our rights, and we are the ones who are afraid that eventually the white apartheid system is going to eliminate our race in this country. The question, America, is who should really be afraid?

Remember how the Republican Party used the furlough of a black man, Willie Horton, a convicted rapist, to create fear among white voters during the 1988 presidential campaign? Michael Dukakis, the Democratic presidential candidate, while governor of Massachusetts, endorsed a program that allowed convicted felons to earn furloughs. Taking full advantage of a racial stereotype, the Republicans did a television commercial showing Willie Horton leaving prison with a voice in the background saying, "Would you want your president to let this man loose in your community for a weekend visit?" This may not be the exact quote from the commercial, but the use of racism and fear by the Republican Party was most effective in helping George Bush, its candidate, become president.

Sometimes, I actually feel government has turned its back on African Americans the same way Pontius Pilate turned his back on Jesus. Not only did the federal government allow black Americans to be lynched in this country, it also allowed groups supporting white supremacy to burn black peoples' homes, schools and churches. Some of you may think this is ancient history, but these same acts of terror, which are motivated by racial hatred, are still taking place in America today. It was just a few years ago in the deep South that a black man was lynched by the Ku Klux Klan.

A Southern court found the Klan members guilty of lynching this young black man. Although they were found guilty, none of these Klan members were sent to jail. In this case of lynching, the court's punishment for the Klan members who committed murder was the forfeiture of the building, property and grounds used to conduct Klan business meetings and other miscellaneous activities. The building, property and grounds were awarded to the parents of the slain African-American male. The white media saw this as a victory for black people in this area and a defeat for the Klan.

The white media across the country made a big deal of the fact that a black family had received over $100,000 from the Klan after it lynched its son.

This is really just another example of how the taking of a black person's life by a white person is viewed as insignificant by the American judicial system in this country. Yes, this black family should have been awarded the Klan's property. However, justice for the crime of murder in America is not handled on a barter system. If that were the case, it should have been an eye for an eye. The Klan members who were found guilty of lynching this black man should have received the death penalty or sent to prison for the rest of their lives. It was a return to the days of slavery when this court allowed these Klan members to exchange money for the life of a black man. Two hundred fifty years later, the penalty for a white man who lynches a black man remains a slap on the wrist and a small fine.

Black citizens were lynched in areas of the country for allegedly violating laws that had never been heard of in most states. They have been arrested and lynched in this country because they failed to yield the right of way to a white person on the roadway or the sidewalk. In some Southern states, black men were actually dragged from their homes and lynched for such offenses as staring at, or speaking to, a white woman in public. Another offense for which African Americans in the South could be lynched was called being "uppity." *Webster's New World Dictionary* defines "uppity" as being arrogant. Just imagine how many people you know who would be dead today if being arrogant were a capital offense. Believe it or not, a black man in America could be sentenced to death for any so-called crime committed against a white person in some states.

In the movie "Lady Sings The Blues," Diana Ross portrays the great African-American jazz singer Billie Holiday. In a scene from the movie, Miss Holiday, the only black member of a jazz band, was traveling by bus through the South when she needed to use the rest room. The bus driver pulled to the side of the road so that Billie could run into the woods. At that time, most black travelers in the South had to use the trees as a toilet because "colored" people were not allowed to use white rest rooms.

While in the woods, Miss Holiday happened to look up and saw the body of a black man hanging from a tree. Screaming, she ran back to the bus and curled up in her seat and sobbed. Miss Holiday was so emotionally moved by such a tragic sight that she wrote a song and called it "Southern Fruit." Black men were lynched so often in the South that it actually became commonplace to see a black man hanging from a tree, as common as fruit, "Southern Fruit."

Again I ask, why did the federal government allow black people to be lynched in America? For the life of me, I cannot understand how a democratic system of government could allow this type of immoral behavior to continue year after year for over 200 years. Whatever the reason, it must now stop. If there is one more reported case of a black citizen being lynched, all African Americans should ban together and take whatever step necessary to make sure it does not happen again.

Years ago, one of the problems was that the local police departments never investigated complaints from black citizens regarding white citizens who were accused of being involved in a lynching. In my opinion, lynchings were condoned by most local white politicians as a method of controlling black voters in the South. Prior to the Civil War, this kind of behavior would not have been a violation of the Constitution because blacks were considered property. Once the Civil War was over, and black Americans were citizens, the government should have used any means necessary to

ᎧᎧᎧᎧᎧᎧᎧᎧᎧᎧᎧᎧᎧᎧᎧᎧᎧᎧᎧᎧᎧᎧᎧᎧᎧᎧᎧᎧᎧᎧᎧᎧᎧᎧ

protect the rights of the African Americans and ensure the same rights for all Americans that are guaranteed under the Constitution.

As a youngster growing up in Maryland, I listened to my grandparents talk about how white people mistreated "colored" people in the deep South. I heard stories about black people being lynched in places like Alabama and Mississippi. As a child, these places seemed to be at least a million miles away, and I never once thought a black person could actually be lynched in my home state. Being lynched was something that always happened to other black people, and it could never happen to anyone I knew.

In 1966, I started my first year of college at Maryland State College, now the University of Maryland, Eastern Shore, which is located in Princess Anne, Maryland. Princess Anne is located on the Eastern Shore of Maryland about 150 miles from Baltimore City. I lived on the college campus, which is no more than three blocks from the city's main street. I walked this street every day en route to either the local convenience store, the post office or the laundry mat. I met Sam Doane. He was my college baseball coach and a close friend.

What do my days at Maryland State College, Sam Doane, and Princess Anne have to do with African Americans being lynched? It was February, 1994, during Black History Week, that I heard how Princess Anne was the site of a black man's lynching. After being associated with MSC for over 28 years, it was a shock to find that I had actually walked on the same ground as the murderous white mob that took a black man from the town jail and hanged him in the town square.

Once, during a televised documentary on black history in Maryland, I was surprised to see Sam Doane being interviewed. As a young boy, he witnessed a lynching. During the television program, he gave his account of the crime. I had spent a lot of time around Sam, and I never heard him talk about this tragic event. Not only did Sam not talk about the lynching, I had never heard anyone else from the college, the town of Princess Anne or anywhere else, for that matter, mention it.

During the interview, Sam recalled this gruesome event that occurred over 50 years ago. He recounted how a white mob took a black man from the jail. Mr. Doane remembered that a crowd of people had gathered and were on hand to watch the lynching. White people in the town had come to support the mob. Black people had come out because they could not believe this kind of thing could still happen in Princess Anne. Sam told the interviewer that the mob hanged the black man from a tree and then set him on fire. The lynching of a black man was just one of the many reported lynchings of African-American males in Maryland during the post-Civil War era. The fact that at the time I was 46 years old and never knew African Americans were lynched in Maryland after the Civil War makes another strong case as to why the school systems in Maryland should have taught students more detailed black history.

Maryland's justice system is just as racially biased as any other state. Everyone likes to think that his or her home is a safe harbor from all the storms of life, and, when we think about misfortune, it always seems to involve other people from some other neighborhood. People just want to believe that if you never talk about a storm, it will never happen. Listening to Sam Doane talk about the lynching made me think that just a small twist of fate could have resulted in a member of my family being a witness to that same lynching or, even worse, being the victim of that lynching.

After witnessing this lynching, Sam Doane had to grow up in Princess Anne. He married his childhood sweetheart, built a home for his family and started his own business—all in this same neighborhood. How did he adjust to living in the same community with the white men who committed this violent crime? Just imagine having to carry the memory of such a horrible sight for the rest of your life. Every time you see a face from the past, you relive the nightmare.

Fifty years later, Sam can still remember the words of a conversation between a white mother and her young child as they watched the black man burning. The young white child asked the mother what that smell was, and the mother replied, "Bar-be-qued nigger." It was a sickening smell, but, even more sickening, were the white mother's words. Sam Doane will never forget the smell or the words.

After I finished watching this documentary on television, I asked myself the question, "Why was I so surprised when I found out a man was lynched in Maryland 50 years ago?" Did I forget about the white farmer who, because he was dissatisfied with the service, used his cane to beat a black waitress to death in a restaurant in a Baltimore hotel? Did I forget the same farmer was found guilty of manslaughter but was allowed to harvest his crop before turning himself in to serve a short prison term?

Did I forget how angry I was with Maryland's justice system for not sentencing that the farmer to life in prison for murder? Did I forget how the justice system added insult to the pain and suffering of the dead woman's family by allowing this murderer the privilege of harvesting his crop before he went to jail? As black Americans, sometimes we do forget how one-sided the justice system is in America, but, if we constantly keep it on our minds, we would be so paranoid we would not be able to make it through the day.

While I am on the subject of lynching, how dare Supreme Court Justice Clarence Thomas use the term "high-tech lynching" to characterize how he was being treated by a Senate committee during his confirmation hearings? How dare he use race as an issue after he was accused of sexually harassing an African-American female? How dare Clarence Thomas put himself in the same category as the black American males who were victims of some of the most horrible deaths in this country? By associating himself with the term "lynching," Mr. Thomas dishonors the memories of all African Americans who were brutally murdered by mobs of white bigots who support American apartheid. Clarence Thomas has absolutely no idea of what it means to be a black man being judged under the conditions of extreme racial prejudice.

Clarence Thomas was chosen by President George W. Bush to replace the late Justice Thurgood Marshall, the first African American appointed to the Supreme Court, because the President felt obligated to replace one African American with another African American. In my opinion, Mr. Bush selected Clarence Thomas because he was a right-winged conservative Republican and an "Oreo." The term "Oreo" is similar to the term "Uncle Tom." "Uncle Toms," named for the character in the book "Uncle Tom's Cabin," are African Americans who are unable to shake the chains of slavery and still cater to the whims of the white master. "Oreos," named after the famous cookie, are black Americans who are ashamed of their African heritage, and, like the cookie, are black on the outside and white on the inside.

Justice Thomas may have been the Republican Party's choice for the Supreme Court; however, he was far from being the choice of black America. He was almost denied a seat on the Supreme Court because of an alleged act of sexual harassment committed against a black female. If Mr. Thomas had been a student of black history, he would have known that black men were lynched by white men in this country for any type of improper conduct toward white women, and they applauded any report of a black man's sexual mistreatment of black women. Why did Anita Hill make an allegation of sexual harassment against Clarence Thomas? Why did this black female make public statements that would question the moral character of a black male candidate for the Supreme Court? I do not know the answers. Only Anita Hill knows her true motives. However, it is my opinion that Ms. Hill, like some black civil rights leaders, was not willing to just stand by and let a man who she felt was not worthy of this position replace Justice Marshall.

How could black America support Clarence Thomas? According to published reports, he does not support affirmative action, and he publicly chastised his sister for accepting welfare. How could he be chosen to replace Justice Marshall, an outstanding African American, who was idolized by all the members of his race? Mr. Marshall fought against the odds to win numerous battles for equal rights for black Americans. Just picture Clarence Thomas, former head of the Equal Employment Opportunity Commission, enjoying the perks of his upper-class lifestyle and his six-figured salary, while his sister suffers the pain and pressure of raising a family on welfare.

Rather than use the fact that his sister was on welfare to win political "brownie points," Mr. Thomas should have used his political influence to find her a good job. As the head of a large government agency, he could have easily found his sister an entry-level position and assisted her with the necessary training that would have allowed her the opportunity for advancement. During his Senate confirmation hearing, senators dismissed the fact that Justice Thomas smoked marijuana when he was a law student and did not consider this violation of the law enough to deny his appointment to the Supreme Court. I am quite sure Congress would have also dismissed any infraction of the rules that Mr. Thomas may have committed by giving his sister a job. I personally think it would have made a great human interest story, which could have given Mr. Thomas some positive publicity to offset the negative effect of the sexual harassment allegation.

The white apartheid system in America has been responsible for the lynching of innocent black men in this country for nearly 250 years. Mr. Thomas should feel at home in the company of the white apartheid system of justice in America. In my opinion, as a right-winged conservative Republican, Clarence Thomas will never have to worry about being lynched because he will never be mistaken for being black.

Maybe the eyes of justice in America are, in fact, truly blind. The fact that the justice system is blind, deaf and dumb is the only reasonable explanation I can come up with to justify some of the decisions made by the Supreme Court of the United States that interpreted the Constitution. The Constitution did not need to be amended to provide all Americans equal rights. It just needed to have the laws already written in the Constitution enforced. The Declaration of Independence states that all men are created equal and should have equal rights. I am not a lawyer, but it seems to be a very simple statement and easy to understand. All these different equal rights amendments to the Constitution did was support the white apartheid mentality that non-white Americans are different from white Americans.

The same racial discrimination that created a double standard in the social structure of America has also created a double standard in our justice system. After the Civil War and the Indian wars, we should have really become "one nation under God" and ended the double standard based on race in America. Rather than make the black and red man equal to the white man, the government designed a system that was supposed to keep the Native Americans and African Americans separate from, but equal to, the white man in America.

The politicians who thought that "separate but equal" would end racial discrimination in America were probably related to the same people who thought the world was flat. Look at how the white apartheid system put the "separate but equal" plan into operation. The separation part of this plan was done very quickly and with relative ease. White men separated themselves from Native Americans by isolating them on reservations in the most desolate parts of America. The problem was the Native Americans never got the "equal" part of the "separate but equal" plan.

If the white man really wanted to invoke the equal part of this plan, there should have been reservations for white Americans in the same areas as the Indians, so they could share this experience together. I have already touched on the horrors of life on an Indian reservation, so I need not say more about that subject. However, I suggest you read a book written by a Native American in order to get a more authentic version of life on an "Indian" reservation. No one would ever have expected white Americans to give up their freedom and live on reservations. What should have been expected of white Americans was to make the living conditions on the Indian reservations as good as the living conditions in most white communities.

White Americans handled the concept of "separate but equal" for African Americans in this country just a little differently than they did with the Native Americans. Basically, former white slave owners gave newly-freed black Americans the choice to remain on the plantation and live as "free slaves" or leave the plantation and try to make it in the white man's world and end up dead. Although there were many liberal-thinking white Americans who opposed slavery, the number of white people willing to accept a black man as equal were few and far between. Fortunately, there were enough African Americans who had the courage to leave the plantation and challenge the white apartheid system for the right to enjoy all the benefits of being free.

In an effort to keep African Americans "separate but equal," most states created a network of programs for black Americans to mirror the same programs that were available for white Americans. Again, white America had little trouble in accomplishing the separate part of this plan, but they were unable to fulfill the promise of making these programs equal. The white apartheid system established black public schools, parks, hospitals, housing, etc., but the system never arranged for these programs to receive equal state or federal funding. The lack of funding for public programs in the African-American community relegated these programs to using sub-standard supplies and equipment to provide services to black citizens.

The bottom line is that non-white people in American society have always been separate from white people and have never been equal. The white apartheid system, which controls the federal and state government in this country, will never allocate enough funding to minority communities to make living conditions equal to those in predominantly white communities. The funny thing about this "separate but equal" mentality is that it is more expensive to maintain than just plain equal sharing.

From 1865 to 1965, both state and federal governments spent millions of dollars on public buildings shared by black and white people to install separate rest rooms, water fountains and cafeterias. The signs "White Only" and "Colored Only" adorned the walls and halls of public facilities throughout America. Millions of dollars that could have been used to buy new books and supplies to better educate black school children or buy new equipment and medical supplies to help save lives in black hospitals were wasted on extra toilet fixtures because white people refused to use the same rest rooms as black people.

Although I have personally benefitted from the civil rights legislation passed in this country, I feel the time, energy and tax dollars used to develop the 1964 Civil Rights Bill was totally unnecessary. When Congress passed the Civil Rights Bill, all it really did was re-invent the wheel. The Constitution had already guaranteed equal rights to all Americans. Why did we need a special "Bill of Rights" for people of color? What our black leaders did by allowing the government to pass special civil rights legislation was to agree with the white apartheid contingent in this country that African Americans are not equal to white Americans. It is not my intent to discredit the efforts of the great Americans who fought to accomplish the 1964 Civil Rights Bill. I do feel, however, that they should have been fighting for equal rights under the Constitution for all men and not for special rights for men of color.

Chapter Thirteen

There is a popular cliche in this country that says, "Crime does not pay." Yet, organized crime in America is a multi-billion dollar business. Just out of curiosity, take a look at the prison system in your state. Do not be surprised to find that close to 75 percent of the male inmate population in your state correctional facilities are African Americans between the ages of 18 and 45. African-American males in this age bracket make up less than four percent of the population of this country. It is virtually impossible, or on the verge of being a miracle, if four percent of the population could be guilty of 75 percent of crime. How can the Supreme Court look at these statistics and allow this injustice to continue?

If you actually believe that the ratio of African-American males in prison is equal to the amount of crime being committed by black Americans in this country, you must also believe that African Americans control a major portion of the wealth in America. If that were true, the African Americans in the inner cities would be living in luxurious condominiums rather than the rat-infested fire traps that make up the black ghettos. It is a well-publicized fact that most of the black males who are incarcerated in America are locked up for committing an illegal drug-related crime. The violence associated with drug addiction and the sale and distribution of illegal drugs is destroying black communities across America.

It is also a very popular misconception among white people that African Americans control the illegal drug business in America. Although the use, as well as the sale and distribution, of illegal drugs runs rampant through the America's black neighborhoods, black Americans do not profit from the sale of illegal drugs. Most Americans have seen the movies and television shows that glamorize the black drug dealers. Even in the movies and on television, all you see are the black drug dealers with their expensive cars and flashy clothes. They have a gun in one hand and a few hundred dollars in cash in the other hand. This is very little to show from a business that shows a greater profit in America than Ford, Chrysler and General Motors combined.

The easiest way for me to prove that African Americans do not control the drug business in this country is to ask this question: How many of the chief executive officers of Ford, Chrysler or General Motors are African Americans? The answer is absolutely none. The most popular illegal drugs in this country, heroin and cocaine, are imported. Tons of heroin and cocaine are smuggled into America on a regular basis. These drugs come into this country on cargo planes and ships. What African Americans do you know who have access to a fleet of cargo planes or ships? The foreign countries that manufacture and sell these drugs usually exchange them for American-made weapons and other products manufactured in America. The manufacturing of weapons and foreign trade are also areas where black Americans have no control.

Another sure way of knowing that African Americans do not control the illegal drug business in this country is because they have no way to hide the billions of dollars made from selling drugs. It is very easy for white people to establish dummy corporations to absorb billions of dollars in illegal drug money. White people control the investment companies, banks and savings and loans that can all be used as a "laundry" for dirty drug money. You see, white million-aires in America are commonplace, and black millionaires, outside of the sports and entertainment fields, stand out like a fly in buttermilk. My point is, if African Americans con-trolled this much money in America, the Internal Revenue Service would have most of them in jail for tax evasion and not drug charges.

In the legitimate business world, the head of a corpo-ration is called the Chief Executive Officer (CEO). In the illegal drug business, the head of the organization is called the "drug kingpin." Both federal and state governments have passed legislation that makes being convicted of being a drug kingpin a serious offense. In some states, the mandatory sentence for this offense is 20 years to life in prison. Ever so often, you read in the newspaper or see a news report on television about a law enforcement agency arresting a "drug kingpin." The arrest usually involves an African-American male from a low-income black neighborhood in the inner city. Just as there are no black CEO's of the corporations I mentioned earlier, there are no African-American drug "kingpins" in America.

The bottom line is simple. State and federal law enforcement organizations routinely arrest black Americans on illegal drug charges. Have these arrests made any impact at all on the sale and distribution of illegal drugs? In the movie "The Godfather," the Corleone family was concerned that some of the other crime families were going to start selling heroin in white neighborhoods, and they did not want the poison sold to white kids. The other family bosses were quick to assure Don Corleone, the godfather, that they were only selling heroin in the "colored" neighborhoods. If I remember correctly, the response to Don Corleone was, "Niggers are animals, so what difference does it make if we poison them?"

I constantly ask myself if drug addiction and the violence associated with illegal drugs were as prevalent in white communities as it is in black communities in America, would there still be an illegal drug epidemic? You do not have to be concerned about drive-by shootings in white America. No innocent children are being gunned down in Upper Park Heights, Greenspring Valley, Malibu, Beverly Hills, Georgetown or Chevy Chase. Most white people who use illegal drugs will drive to the inner city to purchase drugs from a black drug dealer rather than invite that black drug dealer to their neighborhood. Why is it that a carload of white kids driving in a low-income black neighborhood gets very little attention from the police? While I have gotten lost driving in a white neighborhood, I was stopped by the police at least three times before I found my white friend's house.

One of my most frightening thoughts is that the federal government allows the sale and distribution of illegal drugs in as a means to control the growth of the black population. This statement is backed by some very interesting and very convincing statistics. The average age of men who father children in this country ranges between 18 and 45. The number one killer of black men in the inner cities of this country, between 18 and 45 years of age, is due to drug-related violence or drug-related diseases such as AIDS or hepatitis. Dead men do not make babies. There is also a large segment of the black male population of the inner cities in this same age group that is locked away in prison on drug-related charges. Men in prison also do not make babies.

The black drug dealers of today fit into the same category as black slaves who helped the white masters catch runaway slaves. Just as there was no real profit for slaves who helped catch other slaves, there is no real profit for black drug dealers who sell white man's poison to other black people. The reward for blacks who helped catch runaway slaves was the privilege of eating the left-overs from the white man's table rather than the normal slave rations. The privileges granted to the black drug dealers are about the same. The white drug bosses allow the black drug dealers to live better than most African Americans in the ghetto but never as well as the white drug czars themselves.

Is the 1997 version of the justice system in America better than the 1894 version? The racism in our justice system in America is so obvious that it is fast becoming an international embarrassment. The entire free world tuned in to watch the Rodney King mini-series that was filmed in Los Angeles. The episodes of this popular mini-series were as follows: the Rodney King beating, the Rodney King trial, the Rodney King verdict and the Rodney King riot. Each event in this dramatic saga received a tremendous amount of media coverage. One issue surrounding the riot after the Rodney King verdict, which did not get a great deal of media coverage, was the fact that the National Guard set up a barrier to contain the riot in the ghettos of Los Angeles.

Just as in the 1960's when blacks rioted in Watts, the Los Angeles law enforcement officials were unable to stop blacks from destroying their own communities, and, just as it was in the 1960's, the government of Los Angeles used the National Guard to set up a line of defense to make sure that rioting, looting and burning would not spread to the rich white neighborhoods of Los Angeles. There were two major riots in Los Angeles, and not one white person had his home burned or looted. African-American leaders should have asked the question, "Why not use the National Guard to stop the riots and preserve the black communities rather than just have them set up a line of defense to protect the white neighborhoods in Los Angeles?"

During the early 1990's, there were three rape trials that received international attention. In New York, a group of white student athletes from a ritzy New York college were accused of raping a female student from that same college. William Kennedy Smith, also white, was accused of raping a white lady in Florida, and Mike Tyson, a black man, was accused of raping a Miss Black America contestant in Indiana. Of these three heralded rape cases, only Mike Tyson was found guilty, and only Mike Tyson went to jail.

There were two major differences in these three rape cases. The first, and most obvious, is the fact that Mike Tyson is an African American, and the other accused rapists are white. The other major difference in theses case is the venue in which the trials were held. William Kennedy Smith's trial was held in an upper middle-class community, which was very tolerant of the misbehavior of the so-called "rich and famous." The trial of the accused rapists, male student athletes versus female college student, was held in New York City. Felonies are so commonplace in New York that it is very difficult to get a conviction unless the victim suffers visible physical injuries.

Mike Tyson's trial was held in the heart of the "Bible Belt." His rape trial being held in Indianapolis compares to the Scottsboro Boys' rape trial being held in Alabama. It was impossible for the Scottsboro Boys to get a fair trial in Alabama, and the same holds true for Mike Tyson in Indiana. There was no way Mike Tyson could ever face a jury of his peers. The Tyson rape trial should have been held in a predominantly black jurisdiction such as Gary, Indiana. Although Tyson was accused of raping a black female, she was immediately associated with the white daughter of every white farmer in Indiana. These white Indiana citizens, most

145

of them farmers, felt this famous, big, rich, immoral black man took advantage of a poor little innocent Christian girl. The attitude in this community was, "How dare Mike Tyson think he could rape one of our daughters just because he is a rich black man?"

Some of the questions these farmers forgot to ask before passing judgement on Mike Tyson were: Why did Desiree Washington, a Miss Black America contestant and a nice Christian girl, leave her hotel room at such a late hour without a chaperone? With Mike Tyson's much-publicized reputation for physically abusing and blatantly disrespecting black women, why would Desiree Washington go anywhere with Tyson? Why was she in Mike Tyson's hotel room at 2 a.m.? If an adult jumps a fence that is clearly marked "Beware of Dog" and that adult sustains a dog bite, does society want to kill the dog? When Desiree Washington met Tyson, he had a big sign around his neck "Beware of Pit Bull," and she chose to ignore that sign. Why did the system put this pit bull in jail?

The only logical answer to this question is that Mike Tyson is an African American. He being found guilty of rape is just another case of the white apartheid system putting the African-American male in his place. Was Tyson actually guilty of rape? Personally, because I have three daughters, I feel any man found guilty, beyond any shadow of doubt, should be publicly castrated. I would like to make it perfectly clear that I find no pleasure in defending Tyson. He has a terrible reputation of abuse and disrespect for black women which, in my opinion, is a very disgusting character flaw. However, the circumstances surrounding the Tyson rape case should have created the shadow of a doubt necessary to find him not guilty.

The justice system in this country has undergone many changes from one generation to the next, but to answer the question as to whether it has improved leaves me hard-pressed for an answer. An African American has been appointed to serve on the Supreme Court, and, although America has a black Supreme Court justice, black Americans are still in danger of being lynched by white mobs in some states. How could the federal government tolerate anyone being lynched in this day and age? America takes pride in the fact that we have the best educational system in the world, which develops some of the best minds in the world and gives this country high marks as far as our overall intelligence is concerned. Intelligent people do not hang a man by the neck until he is dead without allowing that man the right to due process under the law.

In my opinion, the fact that it is possible for black Americans to be lynched in this country, more than 130 years after the Emancipation Proclamation, is because the white apartheid system supports this kind of behavior. The prison systems in this country are filled with African-American males. Therefore, it should come as no surprise that the majority of the men on "death row" in America are black. It is very easy for white Americans to support capital punishment because the chances of a white American being executed are far less than that of a member of a minority race. During his quest for the White House in 1992, President Bill Clinton was heavily supported by the African-American population. To his credit, Mr. Clinton has appointed more blacks, Hispanics and women to his Cabinet than any other president in the history of this country. However, the appointment of Janet Reno as attorney general was a slap in the face to the black Americans who supported him during his election.

Ms. Reno had an excellent record as a prosecutor in Florida. Included in that record is the fact that she was directly responsible for the execution of ten men convicted of felonies committed in Florida. All ten of the men for which Ms. Reno got the death penalty, and eventually had that death penalty executed, were African Americans. In a state the size of Florida, with all the violent crimes associated with drug trafficking, you would think that Ms. Reno could have convicted one white man of a felony, asked for a death sentence and had that white man executed. You would think the African-American leaders in this country would have been up in arms over the appointment of Ms. Reno as the chief law enforcement officer in America. Rather than challenge the appointment of Janet Reno as attorney general, Jesse Jackson, along with a host of other black leaders in this country, protested the lack of African Americans at the front office in professional sports.

Why are the correctional facilities in America filled with African-American males? Why would an African American support the death penalty in this country? Is the justice system in America designed to send black men to jail? Of course, I am very aware of the fact that black men do commit crimes, and I do believe that criminals should be punished; therefore, black men who commit crimes should be incarcerated. In the words of television detective Tony Barretta, "If you can't do the time, don't do the crime." However, I also believe there should be equal justice under the law in America regardless of the color of one's skin.

The total number of African-American males in the United States represents an estimated 20 percent of the country's male population. At least 75 to 80 percent of the males incarcerated in 1994 were African American. Based on these statistics, a logical conclusion could be made that 75 to 80 percent of the crimes that are committed by males in America are being committed by 20 percent of the male population.

Just think about it: If these statistics were indeed true,

148

with the increasing crime rate in America today, every black man in America would have to become a career criminal just to maintain the normal rate of crime. We all know that it is impossible for 20 percent of the male population to commit 80 percent of the crimes. It does not take a genius to figure out that there is a strong racial bias in the justice system in this country, and it my very strong opinion that we are in need of a change in the system.

I estimate that about 90 percent of the African Americans currently incarcerated in America today were:

- charged with a crime that resulted from some type of a confrontation with a white person;

- arrested by a white law enforcement officer

- prosecuted by a white district attorney;

- found guilty by a jury that consisted of at least 8 out of 12 white people; and

- received their prison sentence from a white judge.

You may not believe these statistics, but before you dismiss them as inaccurate, visit your local correctional facility and check the racial balance for yourself. If you know any black ex-convicts, just ask them how they wound up in jail.

The correctional facilities in America are full of African-American males because the justice system in this country is not designed to allow a black man to get a fair trial. The criminal justice system in America is dominated by white males: white government executives, white legislators, white judges, white prosecutors, white jurors, white police chiefs and white police.

Chapter Fourteen

The Constitution guarantees that anyone accused of a crime is entitled to due process. Included in that due process is the right to be judged by your peers. *Webster's New World Dictionary* defines a peer as "an equal; a person or thing of equal rank, value, quality, ability, etc.; equal; specifically, an equal before the law." According to Webster's definition of the word peer, it is impossible for any minority race to get a fair trial in America's apartheid justice system. There are very few courts in this land that a black man can go into and find justice being issued by one of his peers.

"An eye for an eye," which is taken from the Bible, is the basis for this country's laws regarding capital punishment. The Bible also talks about not doing "evil for evil" and all men being brothers, but we seem to ignore that part of the scripture. Personally, I think the death penalty is the easy way out for the criminal. Life behind bars and never being able to enjoy the simple pleasures of life is a long, drawn-out punishment that is far greater than death. As a black man, there is no way I could support capital punishment solely based on the fact that African Americans will feel the greatest effect of the death penalty. The white apartheid support groups in America merely replaced the words "lynch" and "murder" with "capital punishment" and the "death penalty." There is no way white lawmakers in this country would be eager to support the death penalty if the majority of the men on "death row" in America were white.

It really shocks me when I hear intelligent black leaders support capital punishment, knowing that nine out of every ten men who receive the death penalty are black.

Kurt Schmoke, Baltimore's black mayor, who wrote a proposal to decriminalize illegal drug use in an effort to save the black inner city communities, shocked me by his support of the death penalty. Mayor Schmoke feels the ultimate crime deserves the ultimate punishment. You would think our African-American leaders would realize that the majority of the convicted felons awaiting execution in this country are black males. The socio-economic structure of America will have to undergo a dramatic change in order for African Americans to have any real impact on the criminal justice system. Black Americans need better jobs, so they can afford the cost of higher education, so they can become better qualified to be police chiefs, lawyers, judges and government officials.

Yes, there are some black Americans who fill the same roles in the justice system in this country as white Americans, but, unfortunately, these African-American representatives of our justice system are few in number and usually located in large urban areas.

Why is it that the United States does not allow Haitian or Cuban refugees to seek shelter in this country? Why are non-whites not allowed the same freedom as our white Canadian neighbors to cross the border into the United States? Thousands of Americans cross the border into Mexico each year on vacation. If foreign immigrants are such a problem, why would the government continue to allow white Canadians, white Europeans and other white immigrants to enter this country with little restrictions?

The reason the laws are different for black and brown immigrants is based on the same socio-economic issues. In the eyes of white Americans, white Europeans and white Canadians all help to promote the economy. On the other hand, whites feel black and brown immigrants are burdens to our economic system. They all wind up on welfare or take jobs from poor white people. Will this country ever stop stereotyping minorities? The different set of immigration standards in this country are based on the real fear by white Americans that America's minority races will one day unite and take over the country.

It became a source of embarrassment when a nominee for a presidential appointment revealed the fact that he had employed an illegal alien and was not providing that employee any benefits. Once this issue was brought to light, it was found that many famous politicians and entertainers employed illegal aliens as domestics and did not tax their wages or provide benefits. It really shows how far we have come as a nation when our some of our most popular citizens in America still have slaves. They just changed their titles to domestic servants.

In 1963, a distinguished black civil rights leader, Medgar Evers, was shot and killed outside his home in Mississippi. Evers's death was called a homicide. In 1968, Dr. King was shot and killed in Memphis. His death was called an assassination. Within months after his murder, Dr. King's assassin was captured, brought to trial, convicted and sent to prison for life. The man accused of murdering Medgar Evers was arrested, brought to trial, and released after an all-white jury could not reach a verdict.

Although the death of Medgar Evers received some national media coverage, the coverage paled in comparison to the world-wide coverage of the assassination of Dr. King.

His death united the black population of this country like no other event in American history and brought America to the brink of another civil war. After the Evers murder was followed by the assassination of Dr. King, African Americans had finally had enough, and they were ready to fight fire with fire.

As a result of Dr. King's death, the white apartheid system of justice, specifically the FBI, the Supreme Court and Congress moved swiftly to form a corrective action plan to calm the unsettled African-American population. Not only did the FBI head the investigation of Dr. King's murder, it provided assistance throughout the country on investigations involving racially motivated crimes. The Supreme Court made favorable rulings on some civil rights cases, and Congress expedited all civil rights legislation that had been introduced on Capitol Hill. The fear of a violent confrontation between the races in America had white Americans ready to make concession to avoid a civil war.

The African-American leaders in this country should have taken advantage of white America's fear of a civil war following Dr. King's assassination. Rather than use the unity of black Americans to demand an end to apartheid, African-American were willing to accept the small advances in civil rights as a victory. The quick implementation of a corrective action plan by government averted a civil war, and, after a short time, the black population of America allowed the country to return to the same apartheid mentality that existed before the King assassination.

Dr. King won the Nobel Prize for his ability to conduct peaceful civil rights demonstrations, and he died a violent death. Like Dr. King, Arthur Ashe used non-violent protests to further the cause of racial equality, not only in the United States, but around the world. In my opinion, Arthur Ashe also died a violent death from AIDS.

Although there were other black tennis players who made cracks in the door of the white-dominated professional tennis circuit, Ashe not only widened that crack, he knocked the door down. The injustice in the case of Ashe was done by the media. The media in this country attempted to "bury Arthur Ashe rather than praise him."

Rock Hudson and Liberace were allowed to die from AIDS without it becoming a media circus because they were white heroes. Why wouldn't the media allow Arthur Ashe, a black hero, the same honor?

Arthur Ashe was able to achieve a Number One ranking and gain international fame in the sport of tennis. This was a major accomplishment in a sport that was supposed to be strictly for "rich white folks" and played at exclusive "white only" country clubs. His triumphs as a champion for racial equality were accomplished in the same manner as his triumphs on the tennis court. Although tennis is not a team sport, young Arthur Ashe fought his battles against racial injustice as part of a team. He did not support the more radical black groups who were also protesting racial injustice, but he used his own style to make clear his total indifference to all forms of racial discrimination.

In most African-American communities, more young people recognize the names "Magic" Johnson and Michael Jordan than Arthur Ashe. However, Arthur Ashe used his own time and money to develop programs in low-income neighborhoods to teach kids how to play tennis. His programs not only provided training, but they provided safe escorts to and from the tennis courts for children who lived in violent neighborhoods.

Dr. King's birthday became a national holiday; therefore, his life and tragic death will never be forgotten. However, and most unfortunately, the memory of the murder of Medgar Evers fell through the cracks, and his life and death have not gotten the recognition from the African-American community that he rightly deserves. Thank you, HBO, for your cable television special, "The Life of Arthur Ashe." Thank you even more for your television special on the death of Medgar Evers, which gave national attention to the murder of this great pioneer in the fight for civil rights.

Some black Americans seem to forget that, just over 30 years ago, a white man shot and killed Medgar Evers and boasted about it to all his white friends and neighbors. Not only did he brag to his friends about killing Medgar Evers, he used the fact that he had committed this murder to intimidate other black citizens in Mississippi.

To the credit of Mississippi law enforcement authorities, it did not take them long to arrest a suspect and collect some strong evidence against Byron de la Beckwith, the suspect who was accused of killing Medgar Evers. The state's prosecutor also presented a solid case that included the motive, the opportunity and the murder weapon, which was owned by Beckwith and had his fingerprints on the gun.

Despite the evidence presented against Beckwith, an all-white jury in a Mississippi courtroom could not find this white man guilty of murdering Evers. The trial resulted in a hung jury, and the murder charge was dismissed. Surprise! Surprise! Surprise! Beckwith was tried again, but the results were the same, a hung jury. He was released, and received a hero's welcome when he returned home.

What did Beckwith do after his release? He continued his reign of terror over African Americans and Jews in Mississippi. One of the first things he did was to assure fellow members of the Ku Klux Klan that he would continue to fight for white supremacy by eliminating anyone he felt was a threat to apartheid in America. According to Beckwith, he hated Jews almost as much as he hated blacks. Shortly after his trial for the murder of Medgar Evers ended in a "hung

155

jury," Beckwith was found guilty and sentenced to five years in jail for fire-bombing a synagogue.

Just how slow do the wheels turn when it comes to dealing out justice for African Americans in this country? Thirty years after the death of Medgar Evers, new evidence was discovered against Beckwith. Only after Evers's wife insisted that it reopen the case did Mississippi decide it had enough evidence to bring Beckwith to trial again for the murder. His attorney argued for the statute of limitations in the case, but his appeal was unsuccessful.

Witnesses who were afraid to testify and failed to come forward 30 years ago because they had received death threats from Beckwith supporters finally decided to talk. The new witnesses provided evidence that clearly placed Beckwith at the crime scene. Thirty years and eight months after Evers's death, a jury made up of both blacks and whites found Beckwith guilty. Thank you, Mrs. Evers-Williams for not giving up the battle in seeking justice for your husband's death.

The resolution of Medgar Evers's murder gives me hope that one day the federal government will reopen the investigation of every reported lynching of an African American over the past 50 years and bring the responsible parties to trial. The government should continue to pursue these criminals the same way the United Nations continues to pursue the Nazis who were responsible for the Holocaust. If this ever happens, it could spell the end of apartheid in America, and the war to win racial equality would be over.

Do you really think that John and Robert Kennedy, Dr. King, Malcolm X and Medgar Evers all being murdered just a few years apart was just a coincidence? If you think that it was just their fate or their numbers just happened to be up, then I would like to sell you a share of the Brooklyn Bridge.

It is my very strong opinion that white American apartheid supporters arranged for the murders of these great civil rights leaders in an effort to derail the "Freedom Train." Beginning in the late 1950's, through the late 1960's, these slain civil rights leaders helped to improve the social and economic stature of African Americans. The fear of the black man becoming their equal always has been the motivating factor for the supporters of white supremacy to resort to violence and murder. As I stated earlier, the Civil Rights Movement was a war, and in any war, there are casualties. To this day, the Civil Rights Movement has yet to recover from the deaths of John and Robert Kennedy, Dr. King, Medgar Evers and Malcolm X.

CPSIA information can be obtained
at www.ICGtesting.com
Printed in the USA
LVHW04s1431250918
591324LV00010B/411/P